Illustrations of Old Bideford

Volume Three

Peter Christie

Edward Gaskell *publishers*
DEVON

First published 2010
Edward Gaskell *publishers*
The Old Gazette Building
6 Grenville Street
Bideford
Devon
EX39 2EA

isbn (10) 1-9067696-21-4
isbn (13) 978-1-906769-21-5

Illustrations of Old Bideford
Volume 3

Peter Christie

Typeset, printed and bound by
Lazarus Press
Caddsdown Business Park
Bideford
Devon
EX39 3DX
www.lazaruspress.com

Contents

In Memory of
Mary Cleaver

Introduction

When I published the second volume of *Illustrations of Old Bideford* I wrote in the foreword that 'In preparing this volume for the printer I have realised I am well on my way to having enough illustrations for a third, and probably final, selection.' Here is that third volume which I hope you will enjoy reading as much as I enjoyed putting it together. As to it being the final one well I think there will be another one as I keep discovering new photographs - and kind people keep forwarding me examples as well. I think this is because local residents are beginning to realise that even their own 'family albums' contain pictures of more than just personal interest. In this book, for example, I print shots from the late 19th century right through the whole of the 20th century. As before I extend an invitation to contact me at 9 Kenwith Road, Bideford EX39 3NW or Bideford 473577 if you have any photographs you think will be of interest.

Photographs have been lent to me by the following people who retain the copyright:

E.Anderson
J.Baker
H.Beer
Bideford Library
Bideford Town Council
A.Blamey
G.Braddick
O.Chope
D.Cole
S.Chappell
M.Cleaver
C.Cock
M.Davy
J.Day
D.Gale
W.Grant
J.Harding-Crook
T.Hatton
K.Hearn
E.Lott
R.Morris
North Devon Athenaeum
North Devon Journal
North Devon Museum Trust
P.Paddon
P.Pester
B.Pidgeon
E.Shakespeare
R & M.Snow
N.Sorrell
J.Swain
J.Taylor
Mr. & Mrs. Way
J.Webb
P.Wells
C.Wood
P. & C.Wright

Front Cover:
In May 1935 Britain celebrated the Silver Jubilee of George V and Bideford staged a whole series of events to mark the occasion. Amongst them was an open air dance in Victoria Park - this wonderful period photograph shows some of the dancers enjoying this unusual venue.

Above: In the previous two volumes of this series I published photographs of costumed characters taking part in the 'Historical Procession and Pageant' held on 3 June 1925 to mark the opening of Bideford Bridge after its widening. In the first picture we see King Edward VII played by E.Smith and his 'pageboy' plus 'Britannia' (Nellie Keen) and John Bull (J.Dymond).

Opposite (top):The 1925 historical pageant above was so successful that just two years later the townspeople staged the whole thing again! This crowded photograph shows part of the procession crossing the Bridge - and notice the keen cameraman clinging on to the light standard on the right.

Opposite (bottom): The three people at the front are meant to represent characters from Charles Kingsley's 'Westward Ho!' Notice how smooth and clean the surface and walls of the Bridge appear.

The Bridge

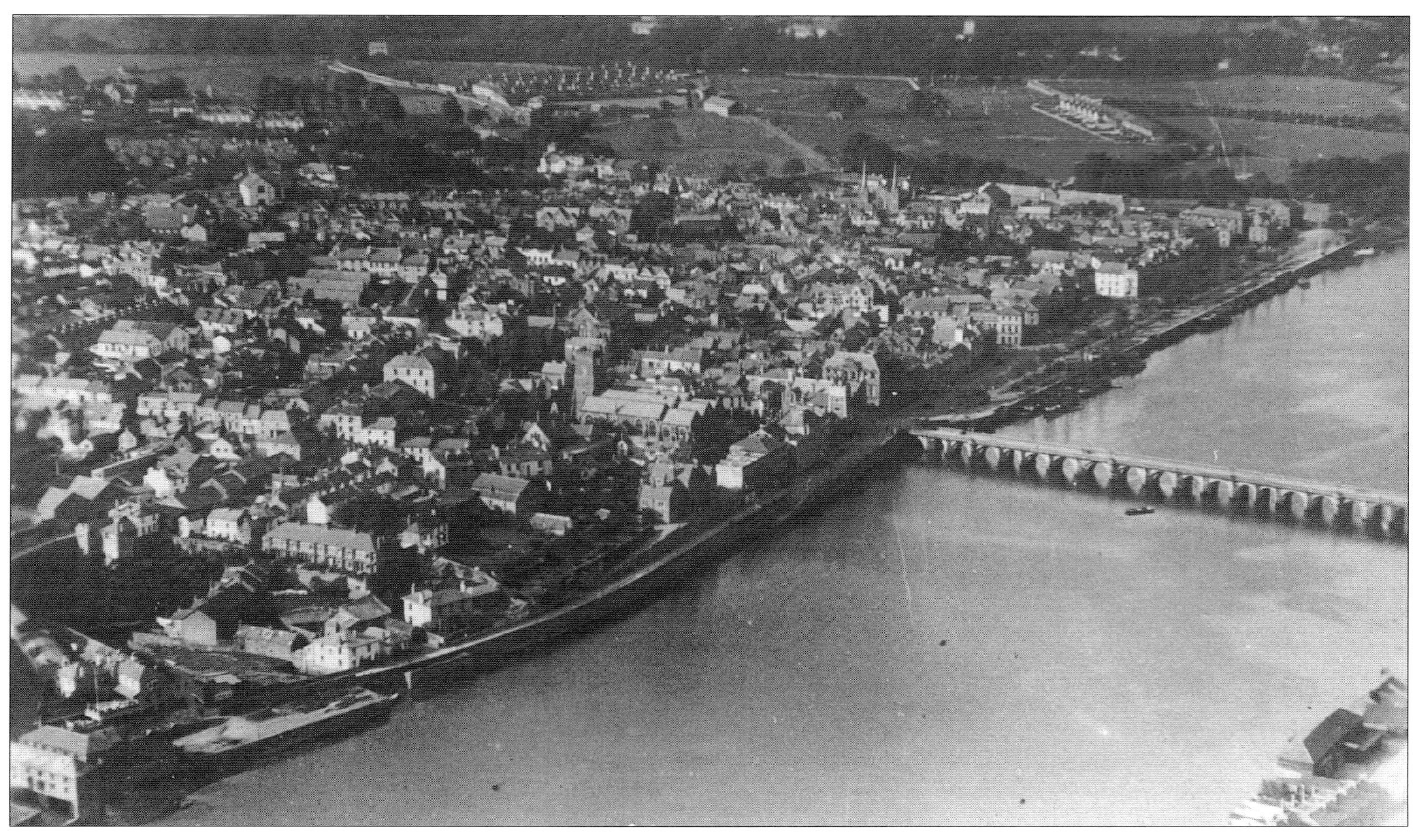

Aerial shots are always fascinating and this one is no exception. Look carefully and you will see Alexandra Terrace in the top centre of the picture whilst the early section of Park Lane is seen to the top right.

The infamous collapse of the last two westernmost arches of the Bridge in January 1968 led to massive disruption in the town - and a long period of rebuilding afterwards. These two fine shots show stages in these operations. The first is a close-up of the steel girders that were put in to support the new road approaches whilst the second shows the large crane that was brought in to aid the work along with the temporary pedestrian walkway (on the left) that was constructed to link the town with East-the-Water again.

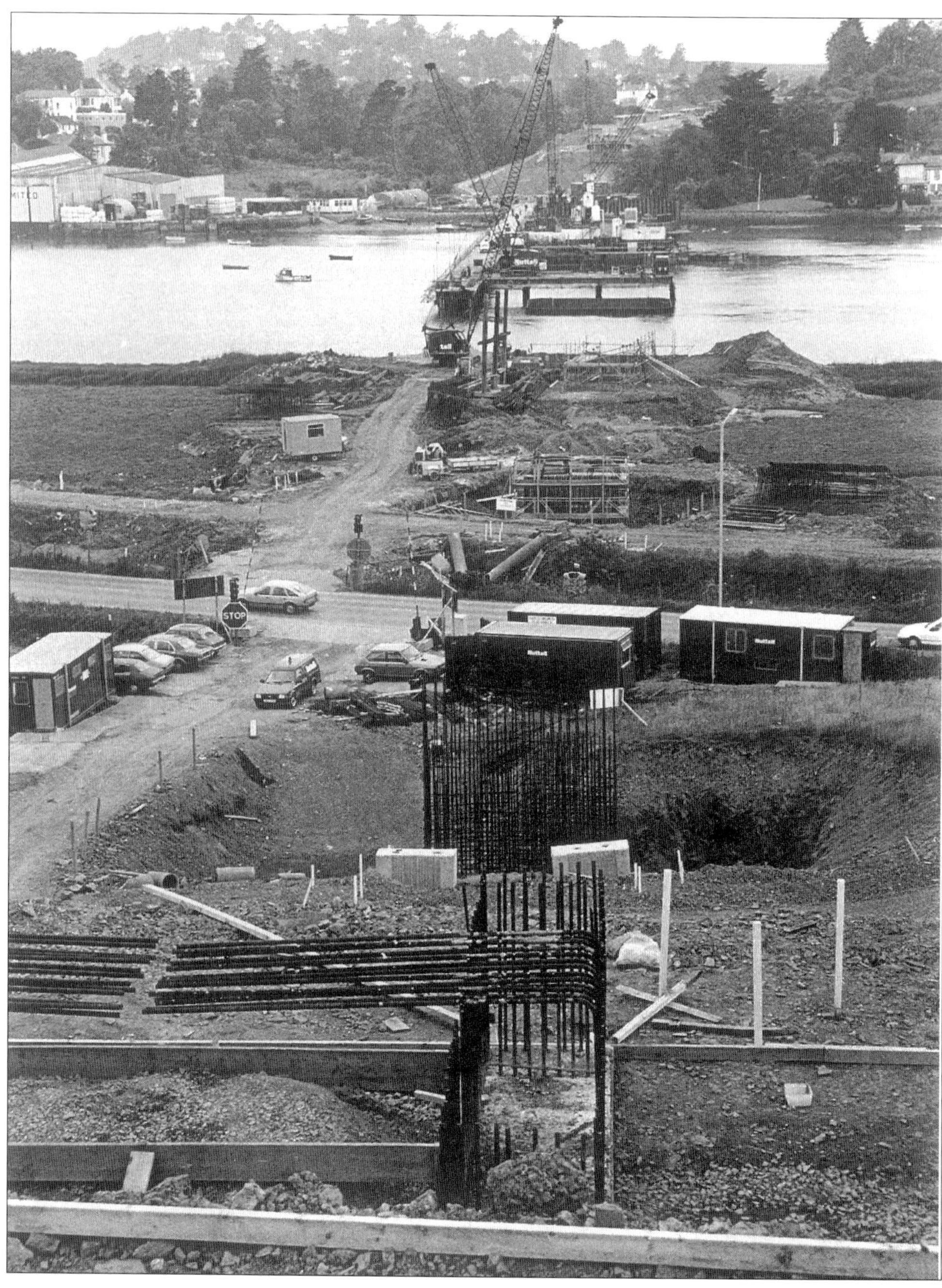

After the last two arches of Bideford Bridge collapsed in 1968 pressure built up to construct a new river crossing - and only 17 years later work began to meet these demands. This panoramic shot taken from the Westleigh side was captured in September 1985 and shows initial work on what became the Torridge Bridge.

This very impressive photograph shows another stage in the building of the Torridge Bridge in March 1986. One of the supports is going up and the two steel beams that would carry the various parts of the road sections are in place.

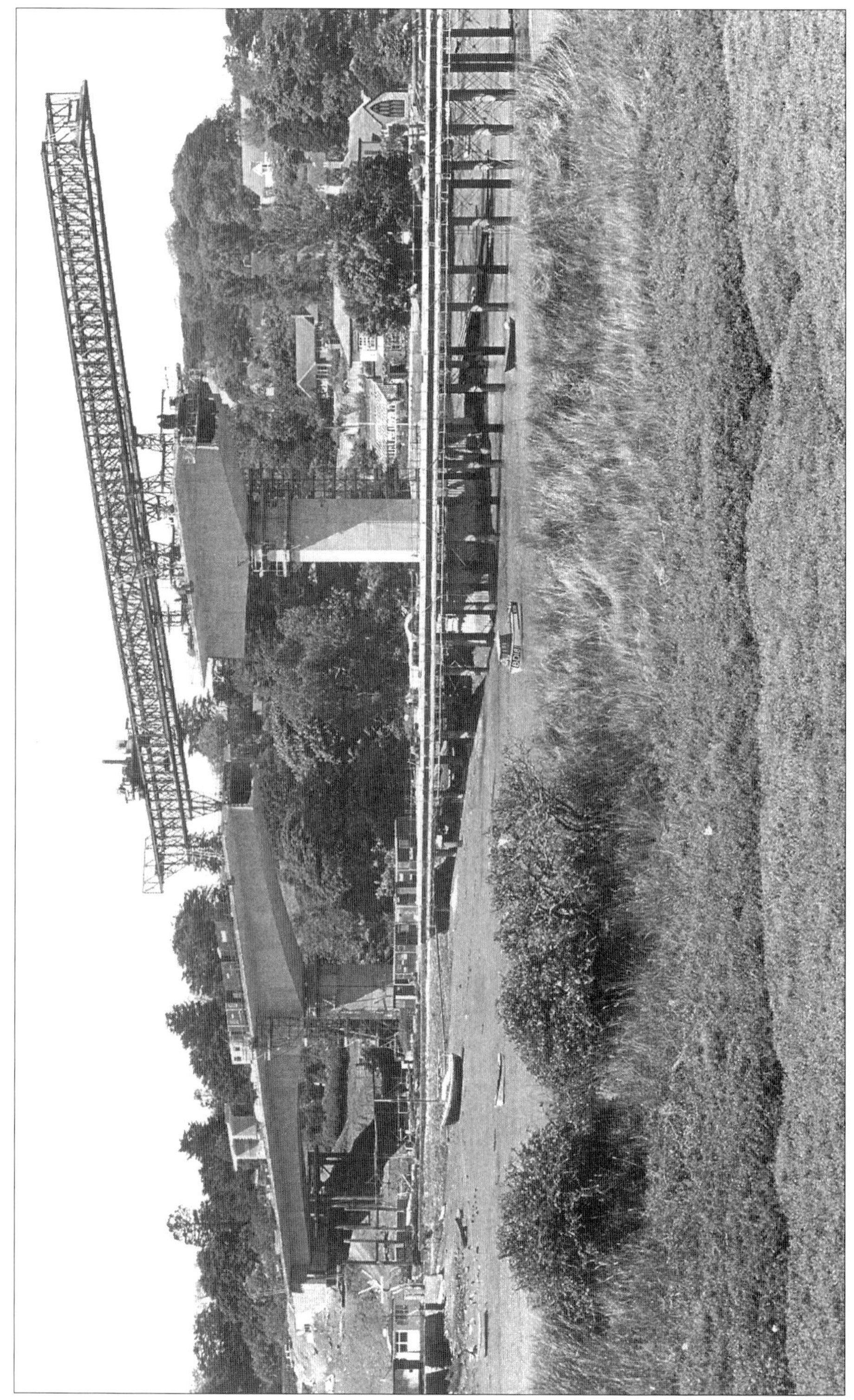

Another shot of the Torridge Bridge being built. The complicated horizontal steel work that carried the sections of the prefabricated bridge out to where they were required is clearly seen in the picture which dates from 1986.

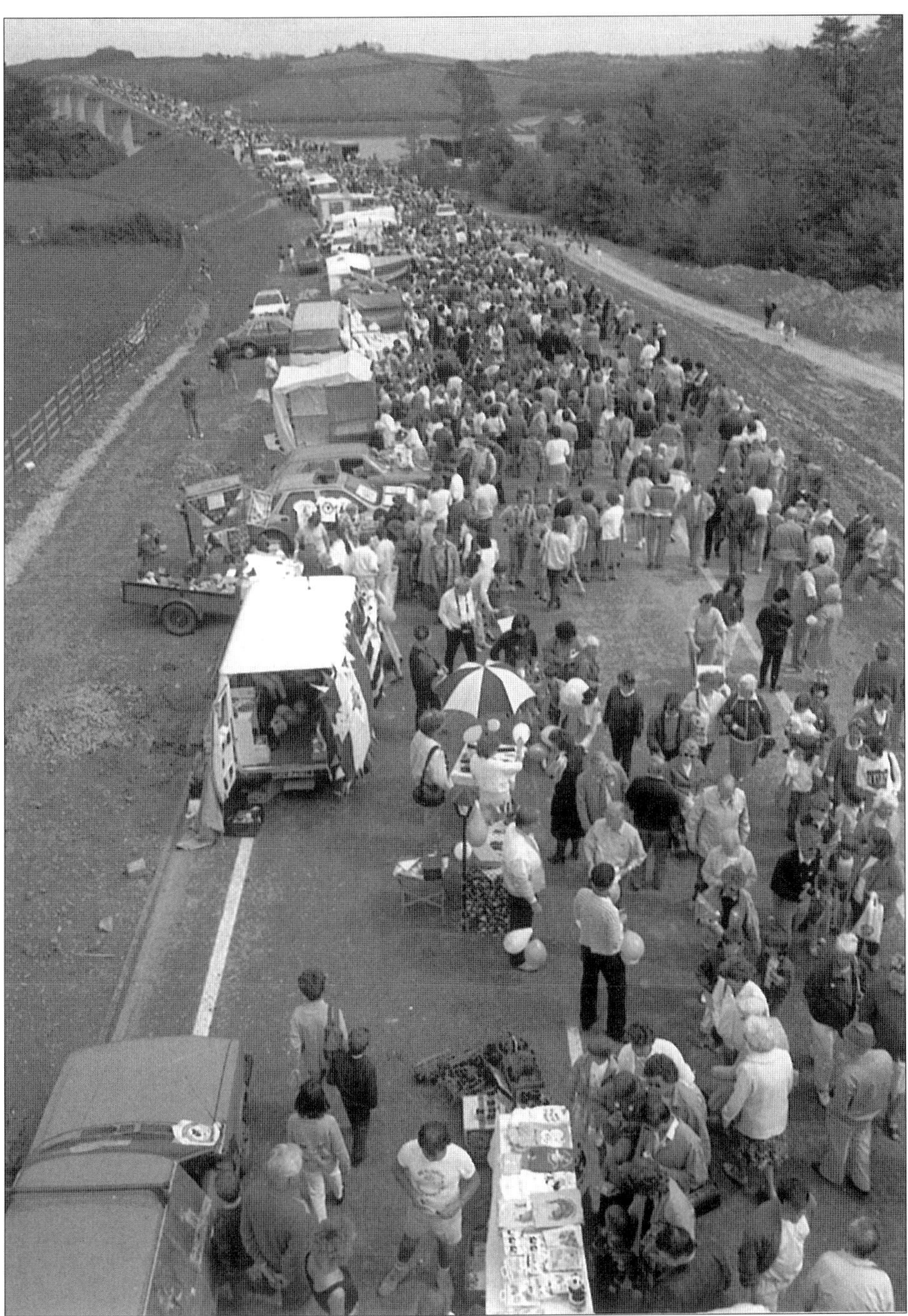

In Volume 2 in this series I published a photograph showing the huge crowds crossing the new Torridge Bridge on Sunday May 10 1987 - the first time pedestrians were allowed to walk across. This is a companion shot showing the various stalls that were allowed to ply their trade on the approaches to the structure.

Shops

Stephens, Brain & Co. ran this splendid looking hardware shop in the High Street for many years. At the date (around 1900) when this picture was taken the shop boasted a huge variety of goods including dog food, hockey sticks and Pratt's Motor Spirit - an early form of petrol. I wonder where the marvellously ornate ironwork on the shop frontage went to?

This imposing shop still stands on Market Hill opposite the entrance to the Pannier Market. The photograph, which dates from around 1900 shows the building was then tenanted by F.Bishop who ran a cabinet maker/upholstery/antiques business there. Today the same building hosts an architect's suite of offices.

What a treasure house this looks! The shot illustrates the interior of Bishop's shop shown on the previous page. It would be interesting to pick out what has remained collectible - as opposed to what has fallen out of popularity.

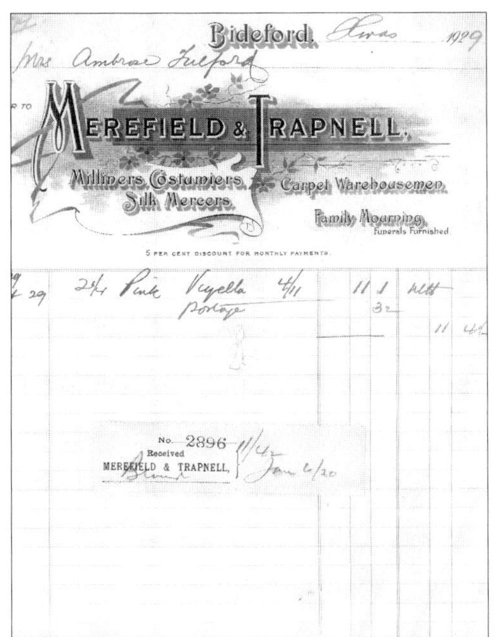

Bideford, Xmas 1929

Mrs Ambrose Fulford

To MEREFIELD & TRAPNELL,

Milliners, Costumiers, Silk Mercers, Carpet Warehousemen.

Family Mourning. Funerals Furnished

5 PER CENT DISCOUNT FOR MONTHLY PAYMENTS.

No. 2896

Received

MEREFIELD & TRAPNELL,

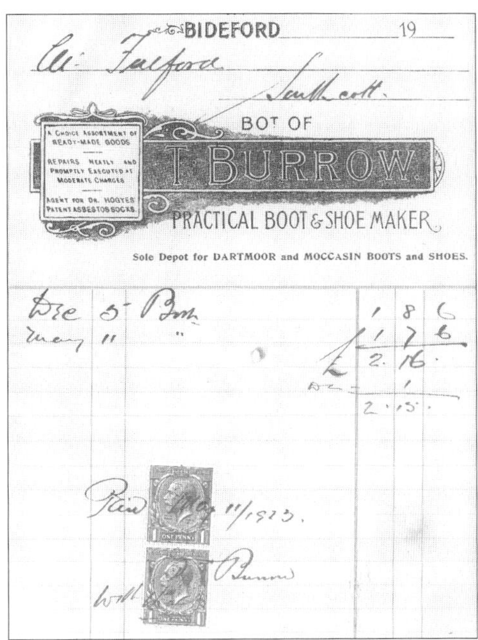

BIDEFORD 19

BOT OF

T. BURROW,

PRACTICAL BOOT & SHOE MAKER.

A CHOICE ASSORTMENT OF READY-MADE GOODS

REPAIRS NEATLY AND PROMPTLY EXECUTED AT MODERATE CHARGES

AGENT FOR DR. HOGYES' PATENT ASBESTOS SOCKS.

Sole Depot for DARTMOOR and MOCCASIN BOOTS and SHOES.

I make no apology for including some more old billheads from long vanished Bideford businesses as I find them so fascinating. Merefield and Trapnell ran a wonderful and large department store where Marke's accountancy office now is whilst Burrows' billhead is self-explanatory.

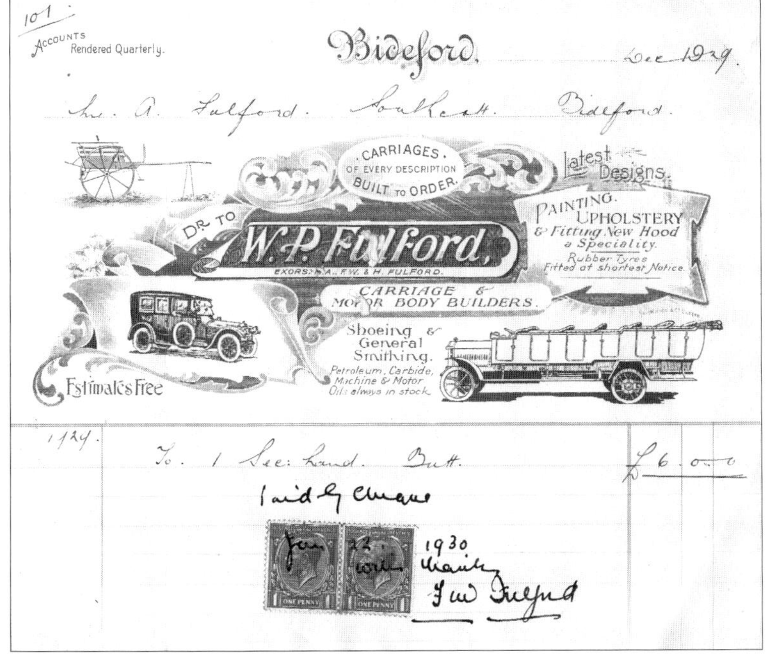

Accounts Rendered Quarterly.

Bideford. Dec 1929.

Dr. to W. P. Fulford,

EXORS OF A., F.W. & H. FULFORD.

CARRIAGES OF EVERY DESCRIPTION BUILT TO ORDER.

Latest Designs.

PAINTING. UPHOLSTERY & Fitting New Hood a Speciality.

Rubber Tyres Fitted at shortest Notice.

CARRIAGE & MOTOR BODY BUILDERS.

Shoeing & General Smithing.

Petroleum, Carbide, Machine & Motor Oils always in stock.

Estimates Free

Paid by Cheque

Perhaps the best is the one for W.P. Fulford's carriage and motor works (with blacksmithing and horse shoeing as optional extras). The hole between the 'u' and the 'l' in Fulford was where it was 'spiked' in an office following payment.

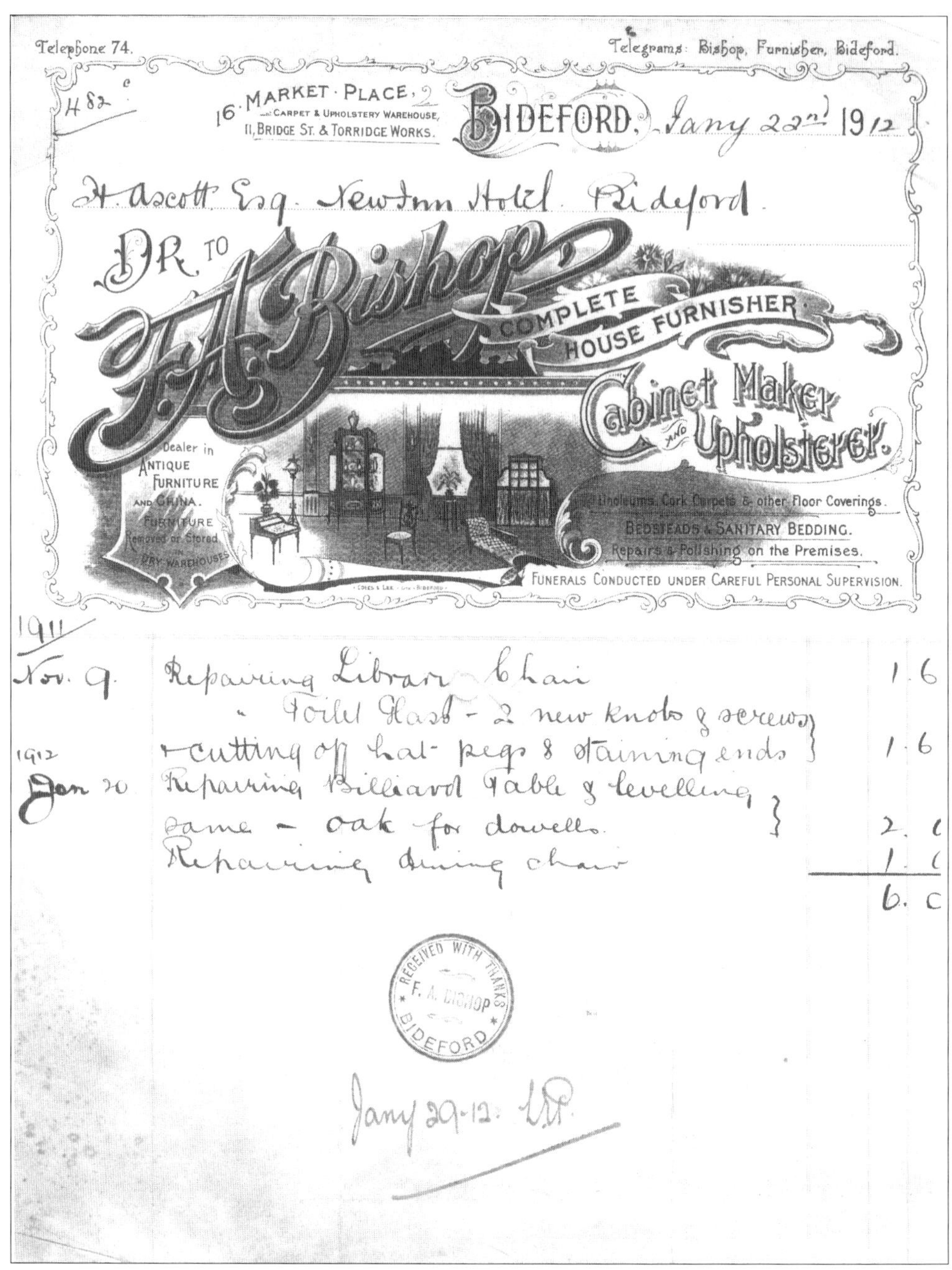

Telephone 74. Telegrams: Bishop, Furnisher, Bideford.

482

16 MARKET PLACE, 2 CARPET & UPHOLSTERY WAREHOUSE, 11, BRIDGE ST. & TORRIDGE WORKS.

BIDEFORD, Jany 22nd 1912

H. Ascott Esq. New Inn Hotel Bideford.

DR. TO F. A. Bishop, COMPLETE HOUSE FURNISHER, Cabinet Maker and Upholsterer.

Dealer in Antique Furniture and China. Furniture Removed or Stored in Dry Warehouses.

Linoleums, Cork Carpets & other Floor Coverings. Bedsteads & Sanitary Bedding. Repairs & Polishing on the Premises.

Funerals Conducted under Careful Personal Supervision.

1911 Nov. 9	Repairing Library Chair	1. 6
	" Toilet Glass - 2 new knobs & screws & cutting off hat-pegs & staining ends	1. 6
1912 Jan 20	Repairing Billiard Table & levelling same - oak for dowells	2. 0
	Repairing dining chair	1. 0
		6. 0

RECEIVED WITH THANKS F. A. BISHOP BIDEFORD

Jany 29-12.

This letter shows one of Bishop's bill heads above an account detailing repairs to the New Inn's billiard table amongst other jobs. It is so decorative one might almost imagine it was worth getting a bill on such a decorated letter as this!

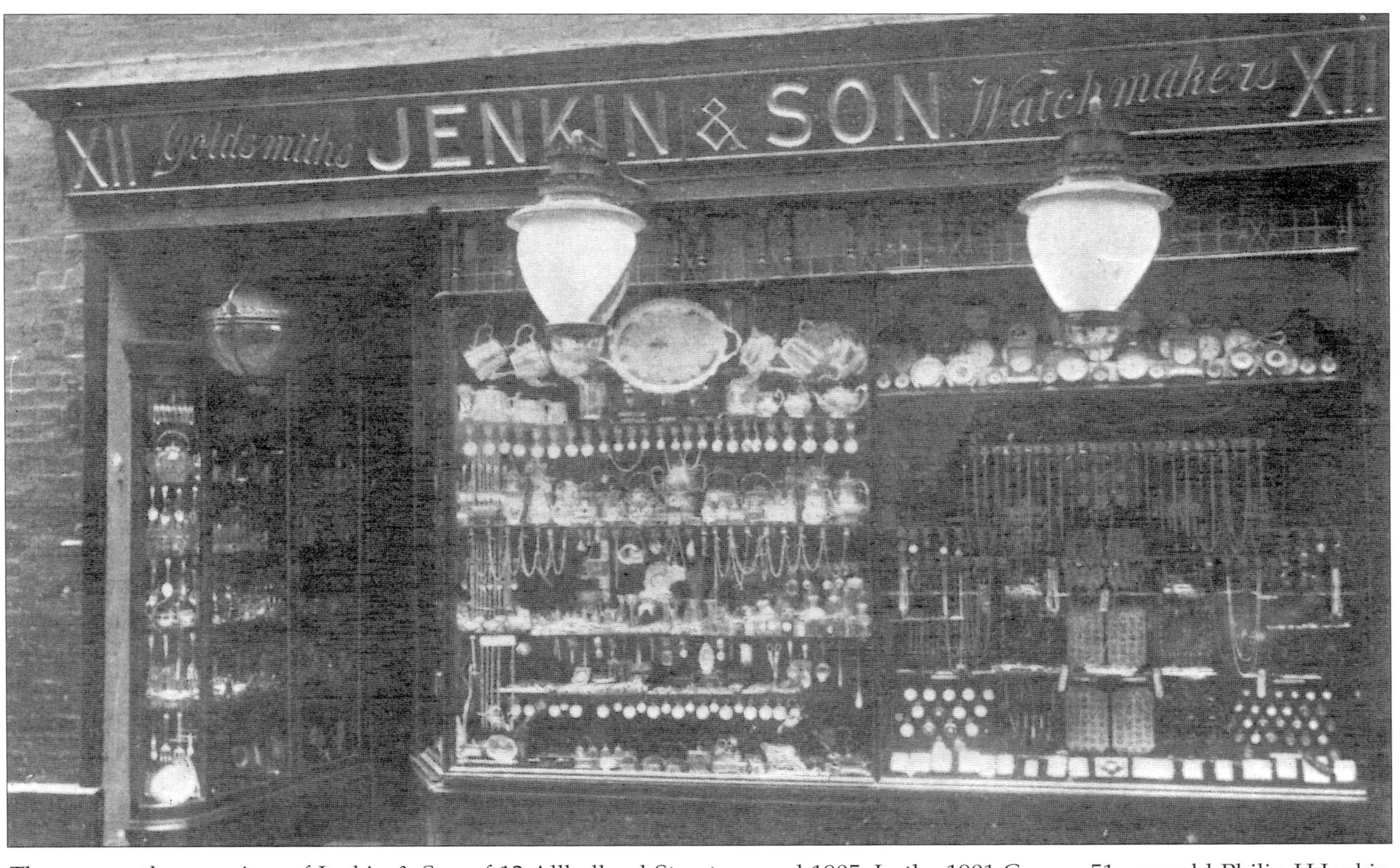

These were the premises of Jenkin & Son of 12 Allhalland Street around 1905. In the 1901 Census 51 year old Philip H.Jenkin and his wife Jane are shown as living over the premises. The shop front was changed greatly, probably in the Edwardian period, and for some years housed 'The Art Shop'.

Dawe's grocery shop stood where Barclay's bank now is on the junction of Mill and High Street. This interior view from around 1905 shows the seats for customers - who would come in and have assistants fetch the goods they ordered - no self-service in those days.

Dennis Andrew's butcher's shop with its marvellous window display is shown here from around 1905. It was situated at 33 Mill Street in a shop that now houses Concept Staffing. The central window and two flanking doors still remains today

Owing to its narrowness there aren't many photographs of Allhalland Street and so this drawing was used in an advertisement from 1906. It shows the bookshop and printing premises of Charles Pearse who had been born in Barnstaple around 1846 and married a Bideford girl. The building now houses Garland's stationery shop - a nice example of continuity.

Next page. At first sight this view appears unfamiliar but the building at the end of the road is still recognisable today - as the florists on the corner of Bridgeland and Mill Street. The photograph dates from around 1910 when the Swan Inn, as noted on the wall painting, was still in being in Mill Street.

E.F. SHORS
PRACTICAL
TAILOR.

The Portobello Inn at the corner of Silver and Honestone Street is one of Bideford's older pubs. In the last few years it has had mixed fortunes but it is still operating today. This photograph probably dates from before the First World War and shows it to have been an unostentatious town pub. Just to the left of the building is where John Wesley preached in 1757

Clements & Sons' drapery business was sited at 74A High Street - which today houses a greetings card shop. It seems odd to us to have so much stock displayed outside the shop but this was typical of Edwardian Britain. The photograph dates from 1906 with the building having been in the long term ownership of the Bridge Trust.

Blackmore's Auction Rooms on the Quay were a notable landmark in the town for many years - certainly around 1920 when this picture was probably taken they were a clearly visible business! Note how empty Jubilee Square appeared with its solitary lamp - not much has changed today.

This was Luxton's grocery shop in Meddon Street in the 1930s. The shop is still there though now it houses a fish and chip takeaway. In the photograph is Nellie Luxton holding Joan Trick. Such small shops were typical in the past before every town was colonised by national chains.

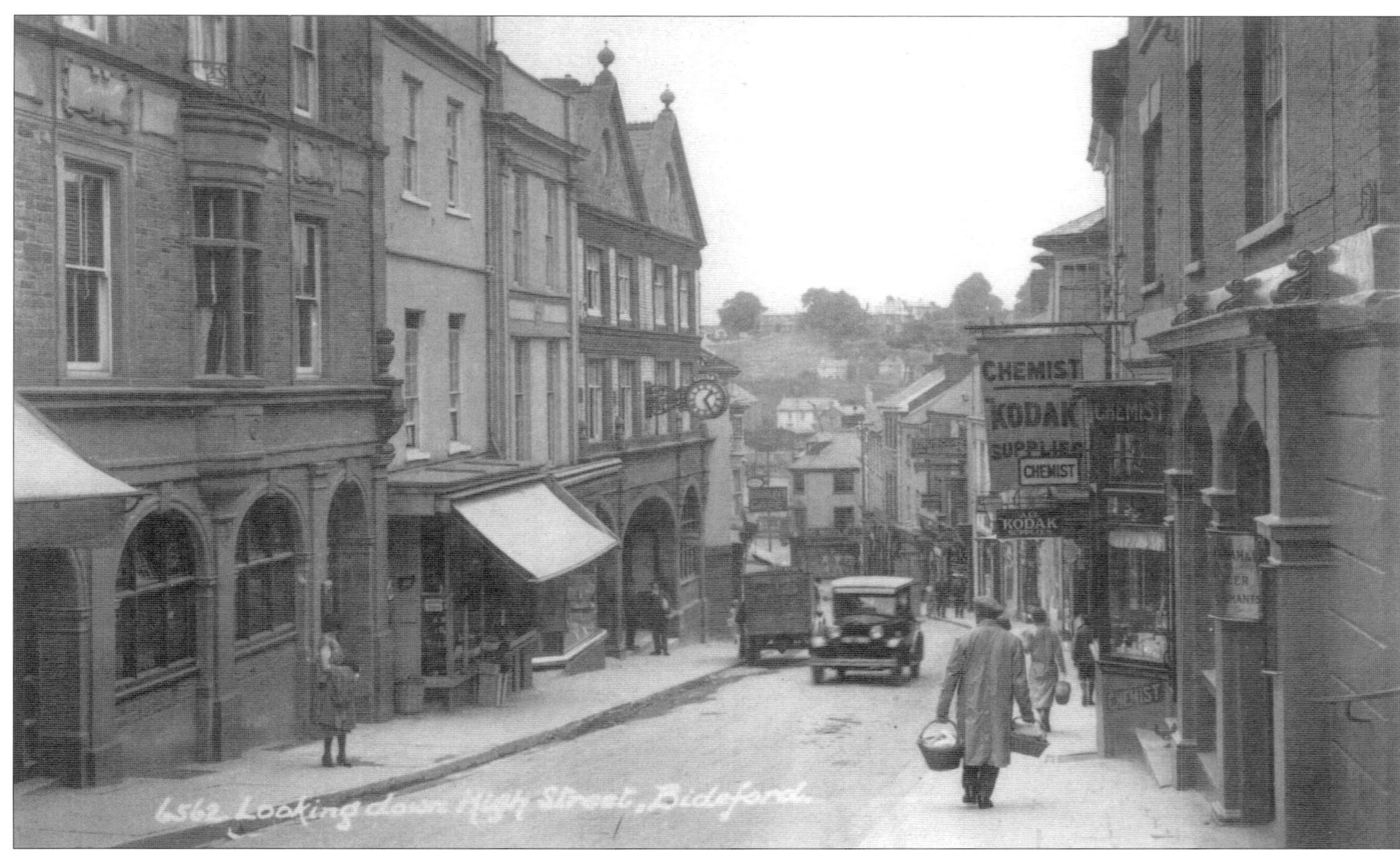

A lovely shot from the 1930s showing the Gannet public house on the left and the Post Office and its clock a bit further down. Note the delivery van outside the latter - two way traffic in High Street was the norm back then!

Not a wonderfully clear photograph but it is an unusual shot of number 45 Mill Street which up until last year was a long running newsagents. In this photograph from the inter-war years it was Pedler's fruit and sweet shop - note the frame to support a sun blind to protect the chocolate on display in the window. The frontage had just been updated when this shot was taken.

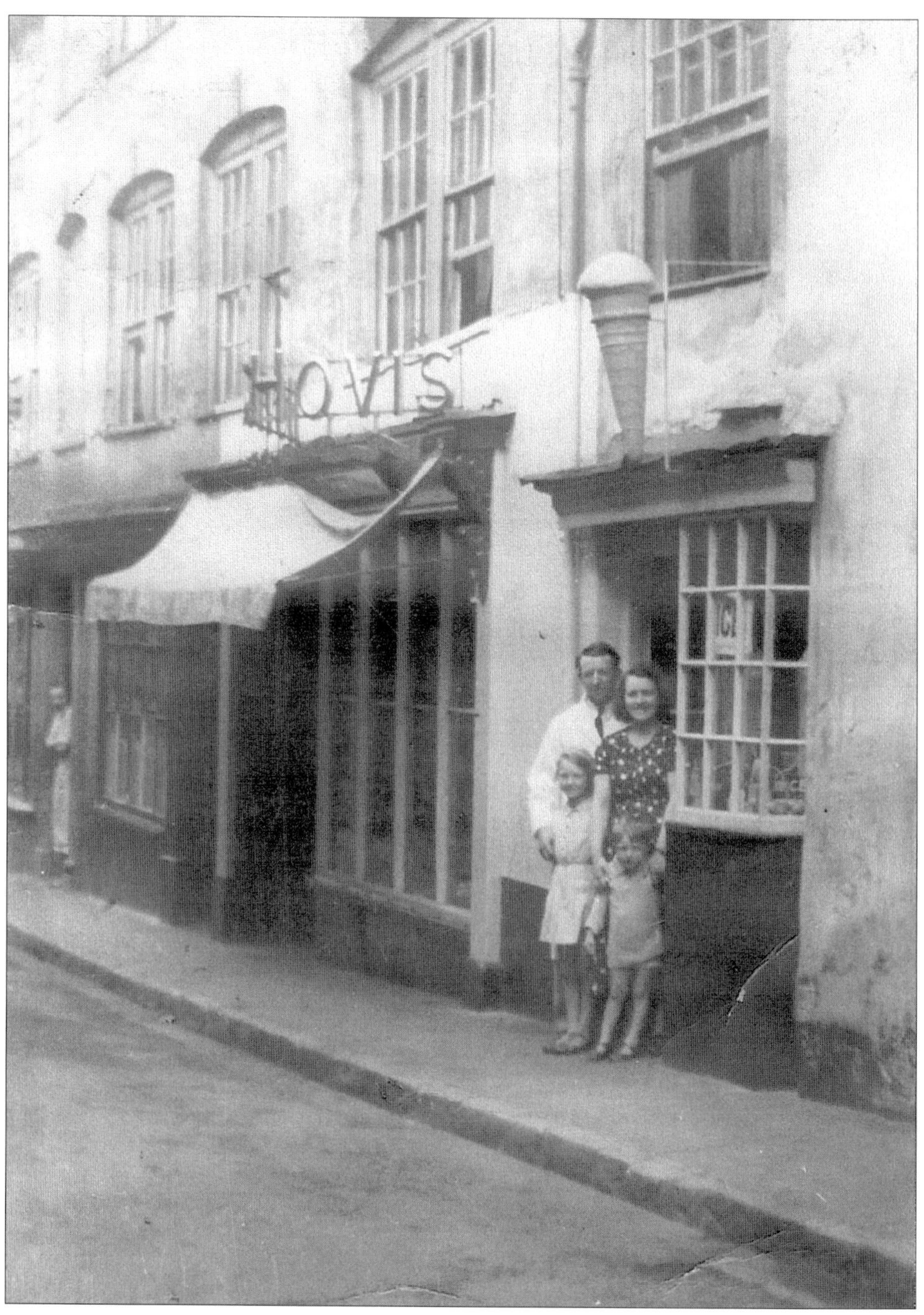

Famously the smallest shop in Bideford this ice-cream business was in Allhalland Street. The baker's premises behind it now house a pet shop. The photograph is thought to date from the inter-war period whilst the shop has now been converted into the entrance to the flats above the present-day shops.

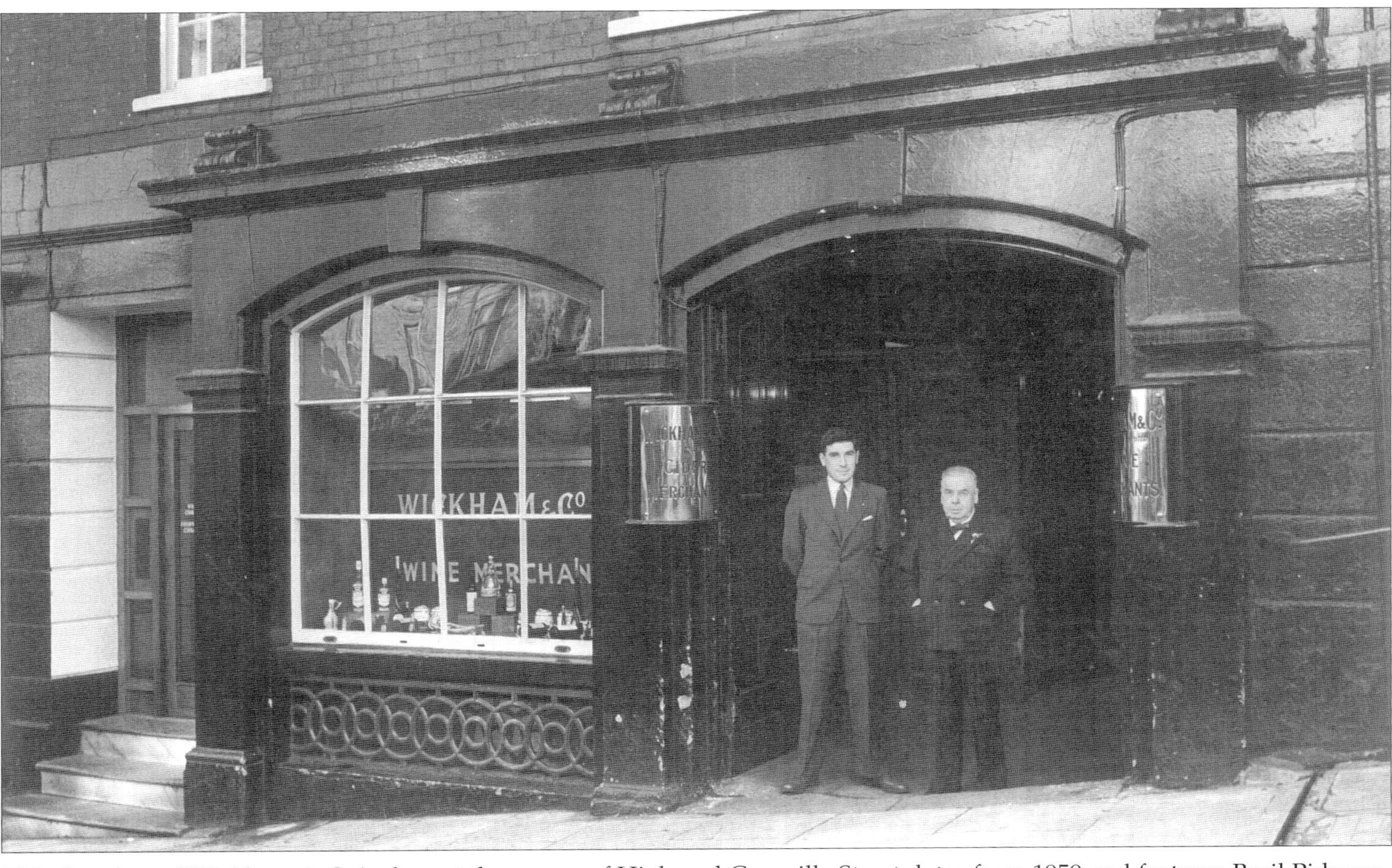

This fine shot of Wickham & Co's shop at the corner of High and Grenville Street dates from 1959 and features Basil Pidgeon on the left with Stanley Fogaty on his right. The Wickham family built these premises in the 1830s and discovered a seam of culm as they excavated the site. This was dug up and sold off - and the family were left with enough space to create a double basement extending far up Grenville Street which still exists today.

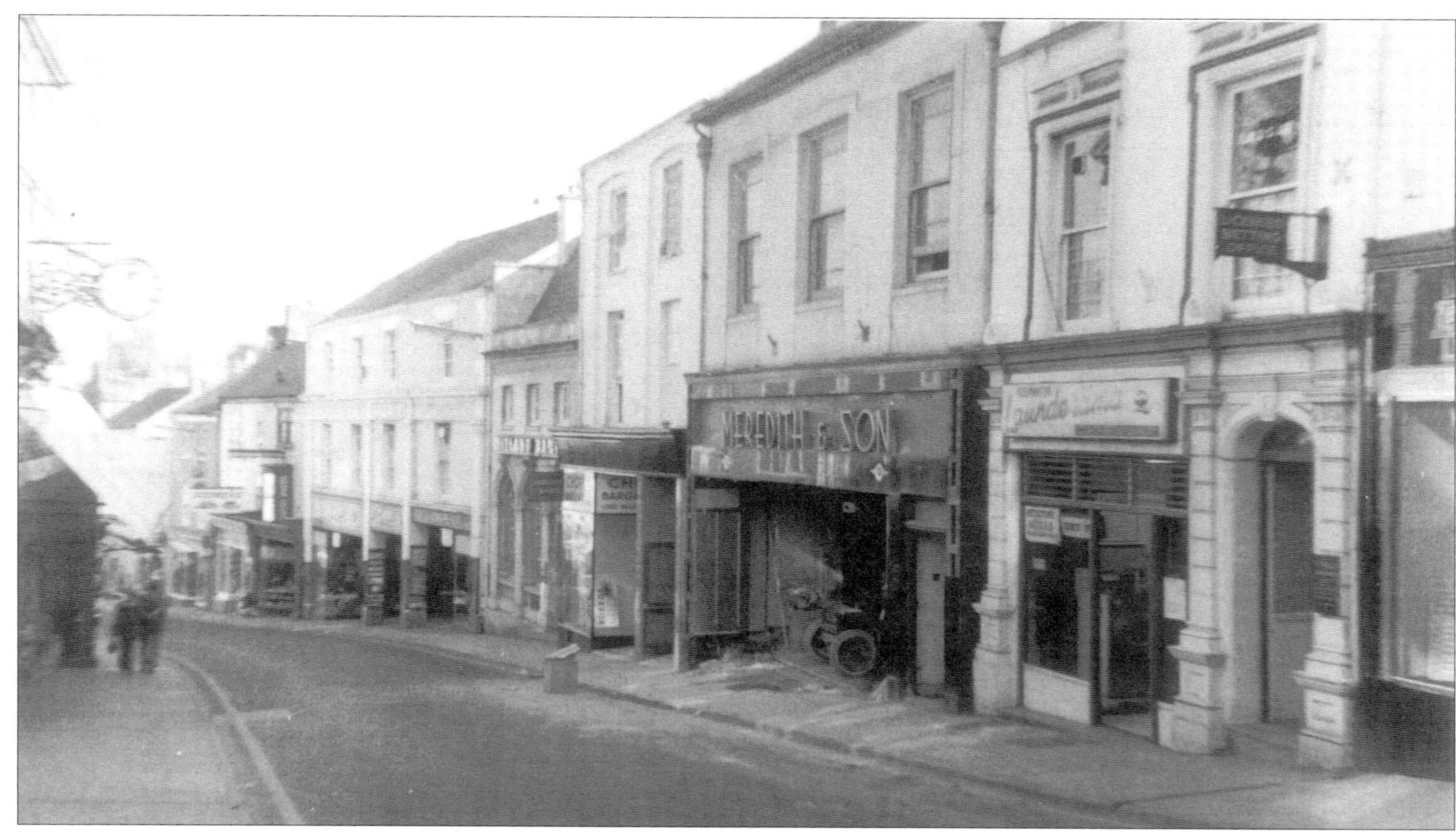

The original photograph is rather grainy but this is an unusual shot of High Street taken in 1971 when the shop belonging to Meredith & Co. was being radically altered. The launderette was already present next door whilst a few doors down the old Midland Bank premises are still in operation - and Chopes has yet to get its new frontage

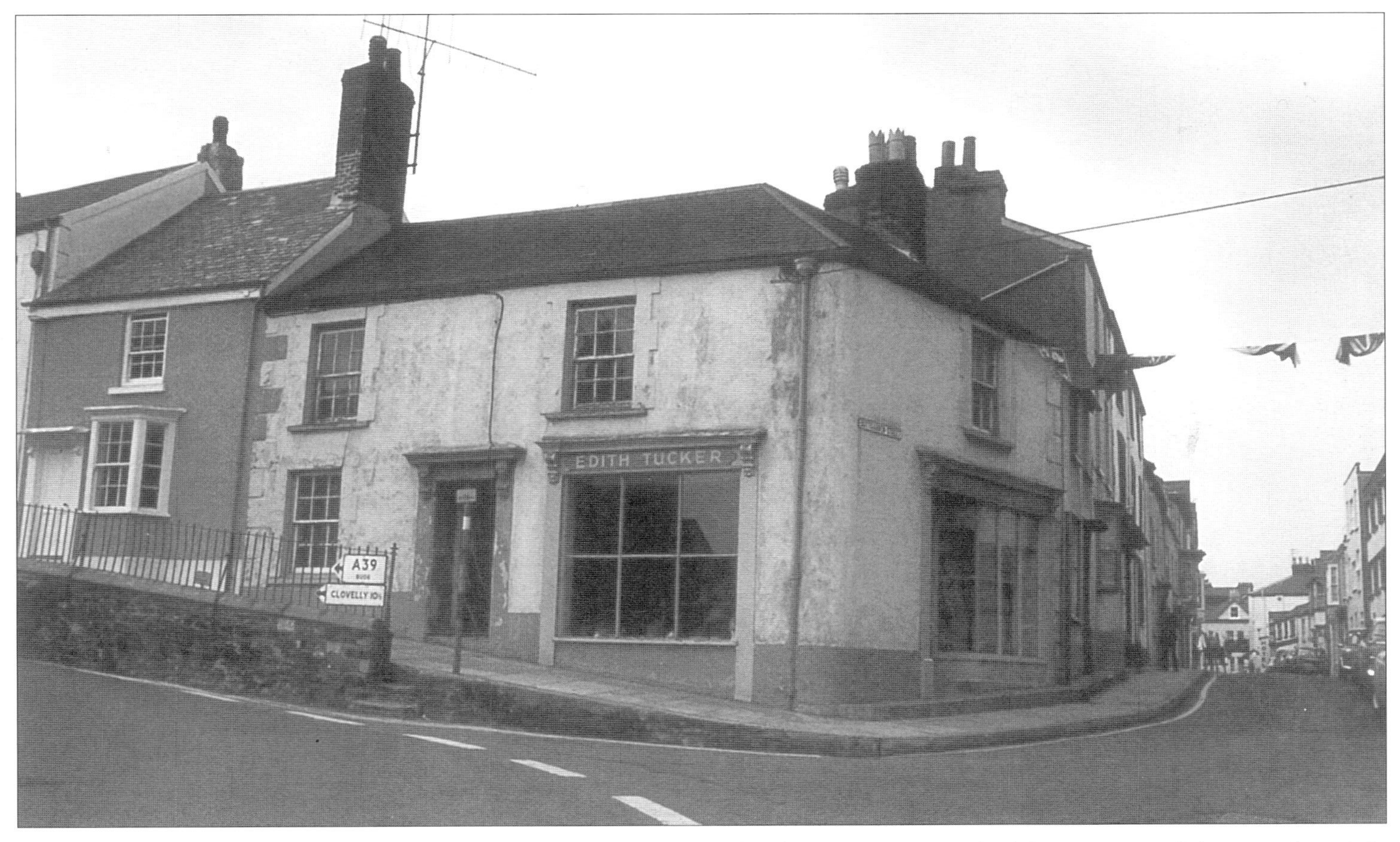

Edith Tucker's small shop on the corner of Meddon and Buttgarden Streets was typical of the many small 'corner shops' that were once found in all British towns and which have now gone owing to competition from the supermarkets. This photograph dates from the mid-1970s before the premises' owners, the Bridge Trust, refurbished and remodelled the building.

Many people will remember this business. Turner's shop was in Mill Street in premises now occupied by Bideford Antiques. The photograph dates from January 1976 and I wonder how many of the articles then for sale ended up in today's antique shops? Notice Gale's Sports shop next door with a long vanished public weighing machine outside.

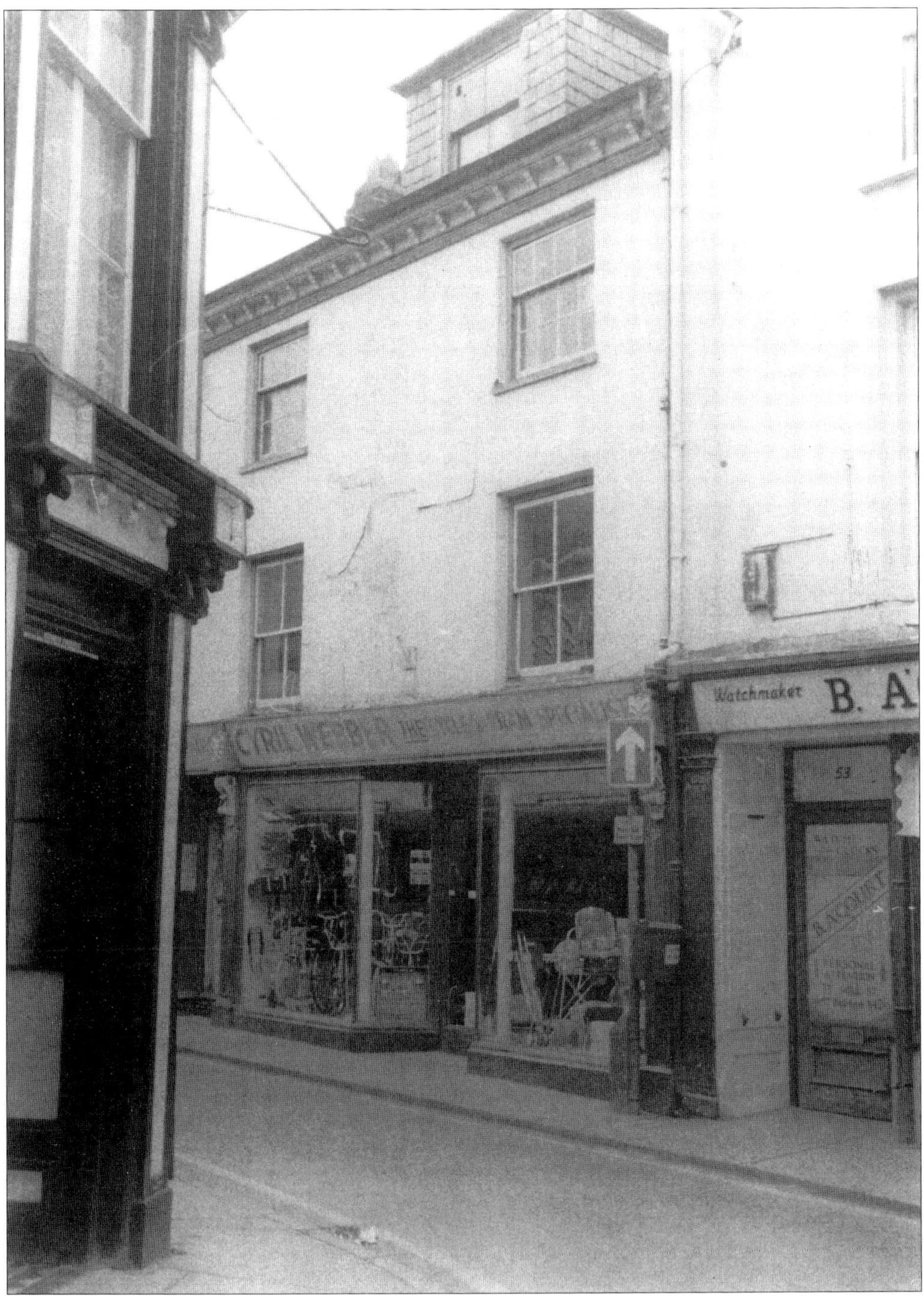

Part of Mill Street pictured in January 1976 which captures the entrance to the Heavitree Arms on the left and Cyril Webber's bike shop in the centre and B.A'Court's watchmaking business on the right - of which only the first still survives.

The presence of the Rose Bird china shop next door shows this to be in Mill Street. Taken in January 1976 the shoe shop window display looks quaintly old fashioned and restrained. Today the shop houses a bakery.

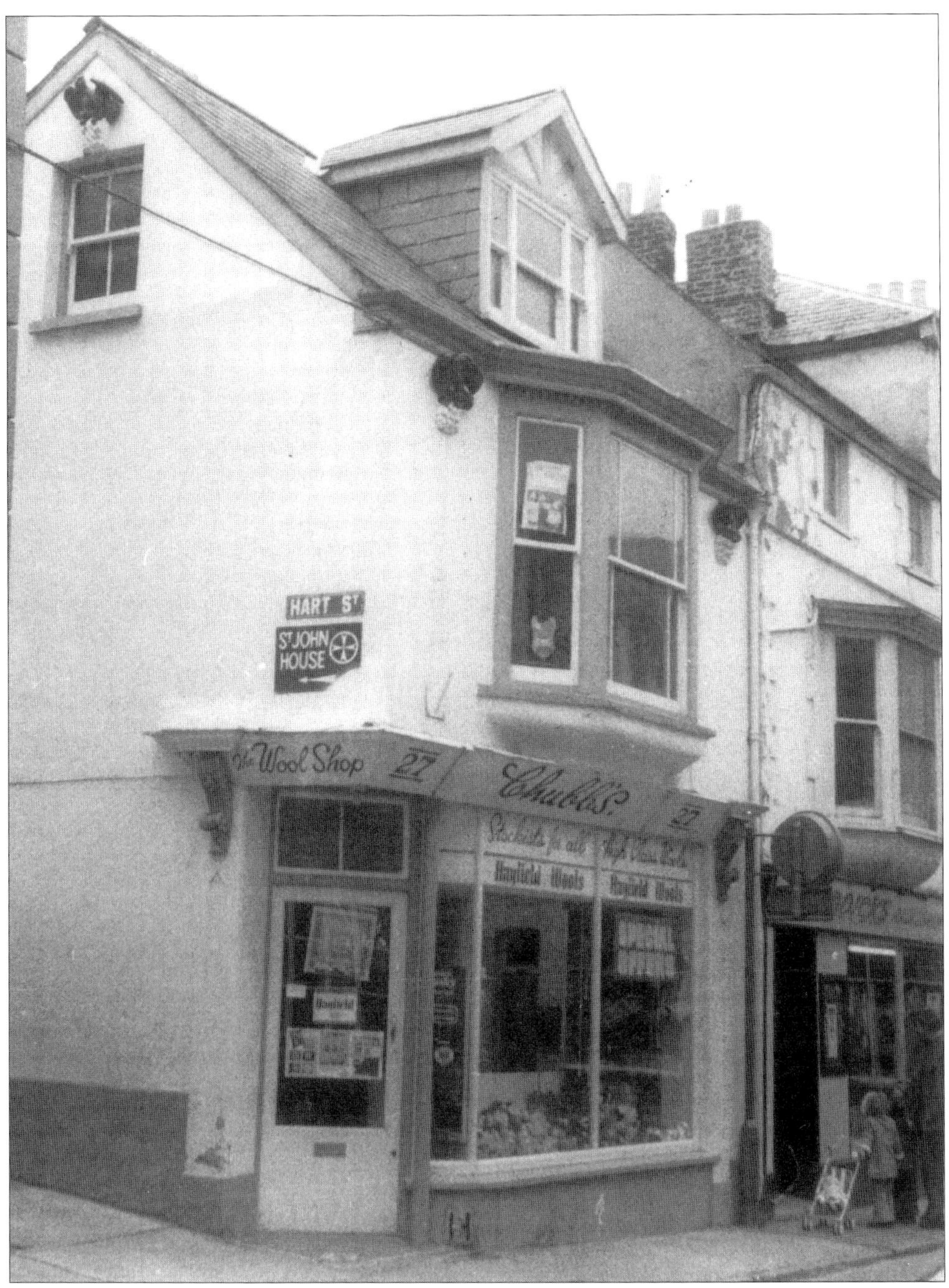

Shops constantly change both their owners and the goods they sell and this one is no different. Today it is a pizza outlet but back in January 1976 when this photograph was taken it housed Chubb's wool shop - with Braddick's record and radiogram shop next door. Notice the stone 'eagles' on the frontage which are still there today and which crop up all over Bideford.

Although this photograph of High Street only dates from the mid-1970s it shows two businesses that have now gone. The Supreme Magic Company was nationally famous supplying, as it did, many amateur and professional magicians with the 'tricks' of their trade. Next to it was Collin's Antique shop with its rococo sign - long a landmark in the street scene.

Buildings

This very early photograph which I think could well date from the 1880s shows today's Natwest bank in High Street. The bank was constructed in 1853 by E.M.White to the designs of Richard Gould. The chains stretched across the Quay were placed there following an accident when a horse drawn omnibus fell into the river at this point and 8 people were drowned.

Overleaf: This lovely old shot dates from the 1890s and shows three of the Quay's four adjoining public houses. The Steam Packet and Railway Hotel was demolished - to be replaced by the Bideford Building Society, whilst the Newfoundland Inn became the Rose of Torridge café before being refurbished as Mr.Chips. The King's Arms is, of course, still there. Note how narrow the Quay was - and the presence of chains to prevent people accidentally straying over the harbour wall at night.

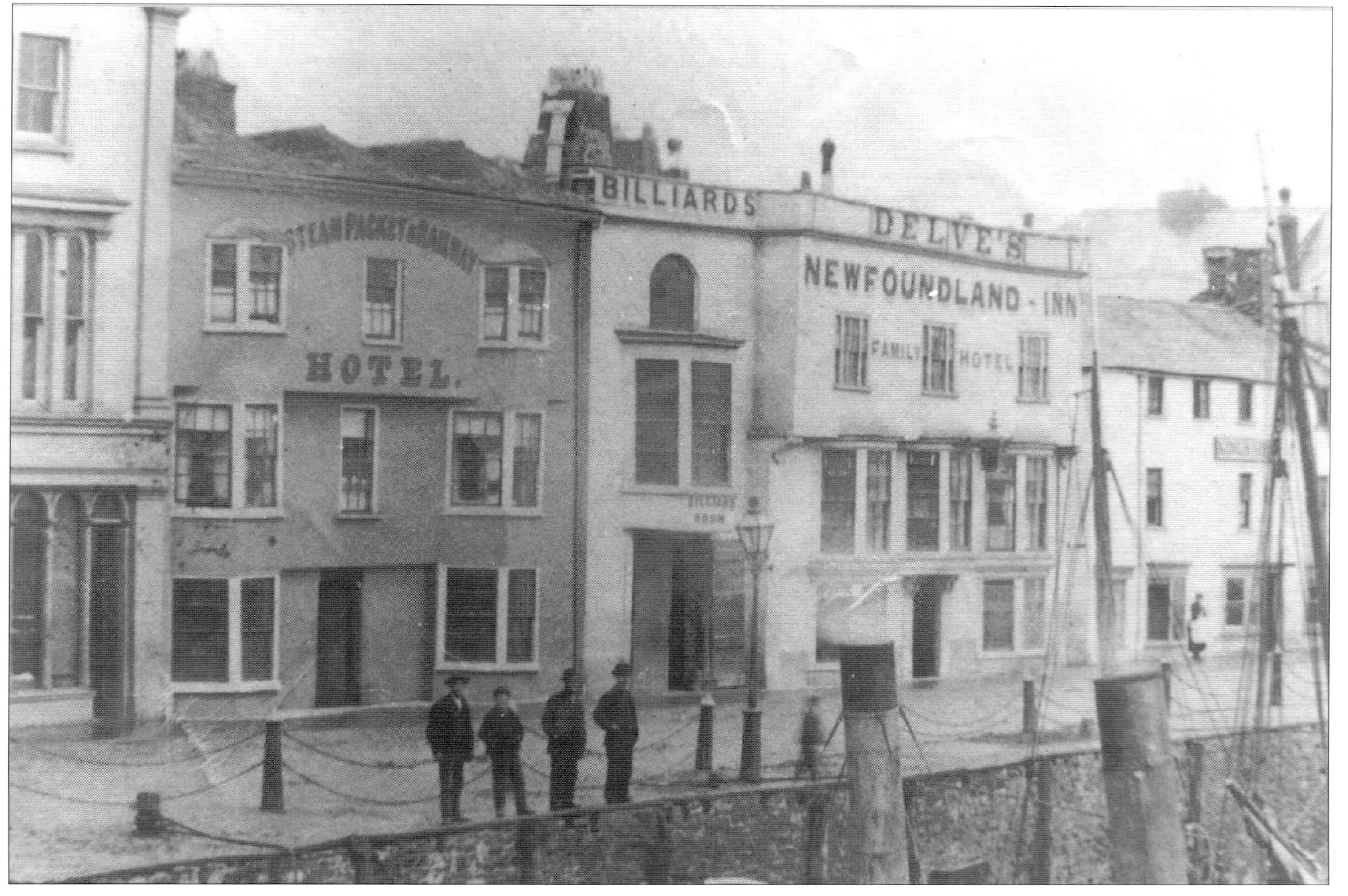
STEAM PACKET & RAILWAY
HOTEL.
BILLIARDS
DELVE'S
NEWFOUNDLAND - INN
FAMILY HOTEL
BILLIARD ROOM

This shot was taken at the western end of the Bridge and shows the shop that existed where today's Bridge Buildings stand. These were built in 1882 so this photograph clearly predates them. On the left is part of the old colonnaded town hall - under which the town stocks used to sit. The photograph was published by W.H.Friendship of Bideford.

Churches don't usually change much but St.Peter's, East-the-Water has become derelict and empty since this photograph was taken around 1910. The small daughter church of St.Mary's was opened in 1889 to replace a prefabricated iron church that had stood on the riverside in Barnstaple Street since 1881.

This corner is unrecognizable today but this picture actually shows the corner of Silver Street and Meddon Street some time around 1900. The small shoemaker's shop was run by F.Squire who was displaying theatrical posters in his front window.

Overleaf: At first glance it would be very difficult to identify the site of this shot - but if I say it is Silver Street where it joins Meddon Street you will probably recognize it. Since this view was captured on a glass plate the steps to the house have disappeared with the whole frontage being moved forward.

HOUSE

This busy scene was Barnstaple Street around 1900 - with its numerous children, its horse droppings and a highly ornamental looking gas lamp. The shop board on the left advertises J.Boaden's bakery shop. In the 1901 census John and Anne Boaden are shown as living here with their son Percival. John was then aged 29 and was described as a 'Confectioner' having being born in Barnstaple.

This fine study of Bridgeland Street shows Bideford's grandest thoroughfare well. A lot of the buildings in the photograph have changed - sometimes fairly drastically. I would hazard a date around 1900 as gas lamps are still present and none of the buildings appears to have been converted into a shop yet.

These two very striking photographs show the construction of Geneva School in 1903. This handsome building was erected to house 1000 girls and infants becoming a secondary modern school after 1944 and Bideford Comprehensive in 1975. The contractor was H.Glover and the second photograph shows the men who actually did the work - note how some of them are holding the tools of their trade - and the apparent rule that every man had to have a hat and a waistcoat.

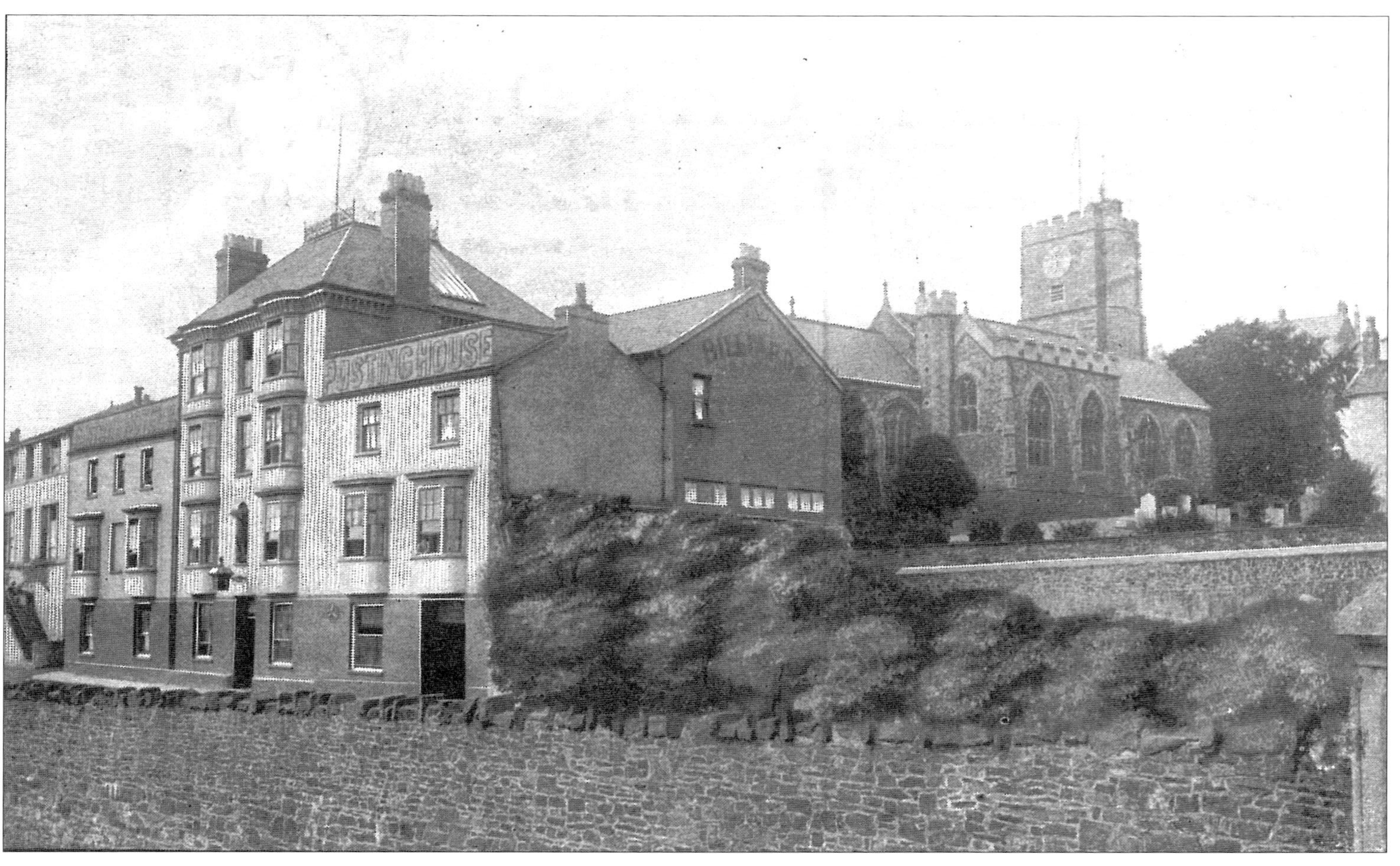

This is clearly Tanton's Hotel but it is a view that was only ever briefly available. It shows the site of the library around 1903 just after the council had purchased the two businesses that once stood there - Pridham's stables and Hogg's the chemist. By 1906 this view had disappeared

These two houses with their intricate brickwork patterns were constructed by J.Cock one time Mayor and notable head of a local building firm who both lived and died in the one on the left. Today, with new shop fronts inserted at street level they house Seldon's and the Alliance & Leicester.

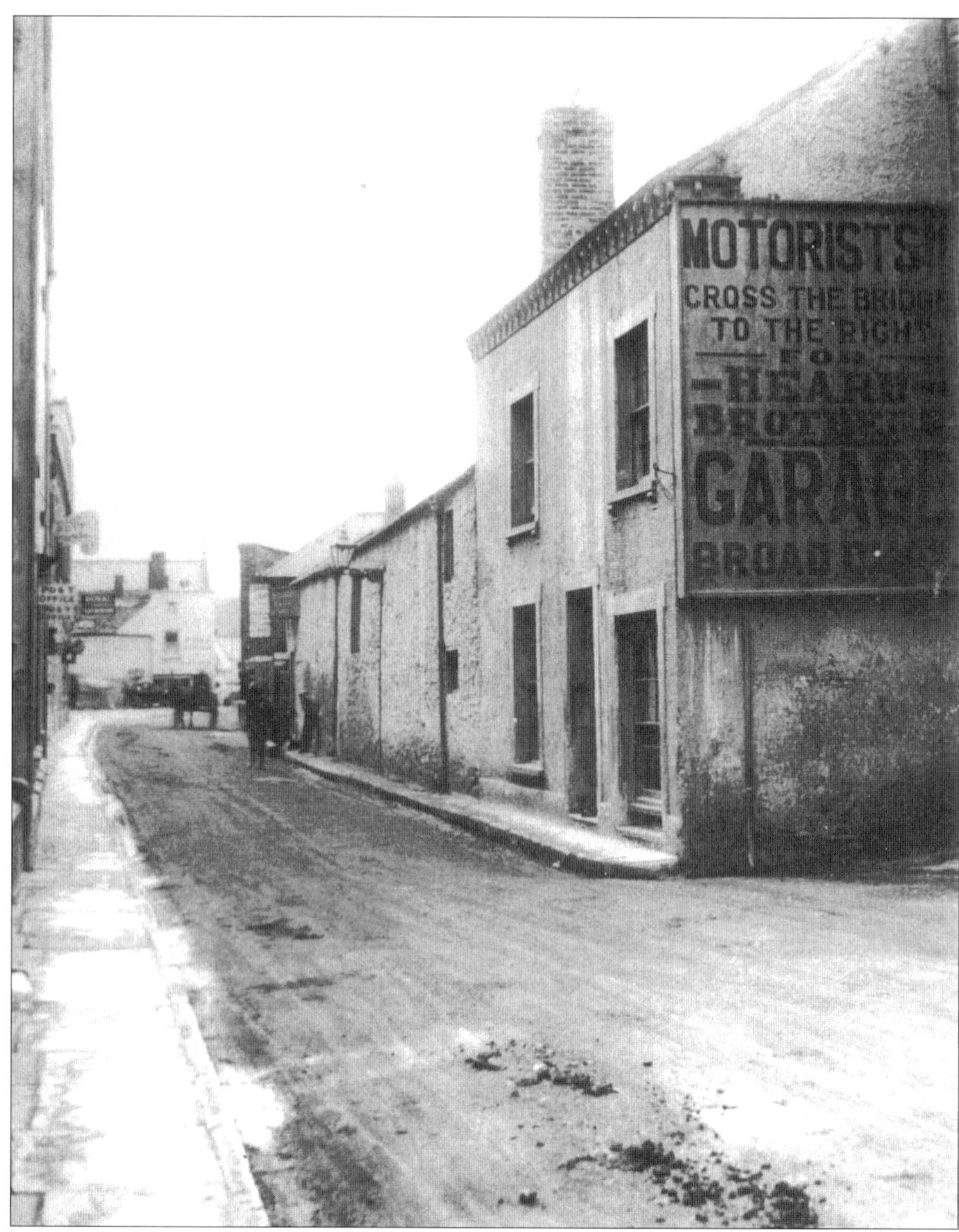

This striking view from around 1910 shows Barnstaple Street, East-the-Water looking towards the Bridge. The huge advertising board for Heard Brothers' Garage is a sign of the time - even if the horse dung in the road seems to indicate that horse transport was still a very common form of transport here in Bideford.

Tower Street en fete here in a photograph which I think dates from the 1911 Coronation of George V. The railings on the left almost certainly disappeared during the Second World War drive for metal salvage but other than these (and the flags!) the street is still recognizable as the small, quiet route to St.Mary's and the Quay that we know today.

This close-up shows two small boys, in their then very fashionable 'sailor suits', standing on the doorstep of the house on the right in the previous picture.

This building is still easily recognisable today as the Conservative Club in Bridgeland Street. The photograph dates from around 1920 and even at that date was a political club - as shown by the painted inscription round the door - either side of the amazingly ornate gas lamp.

This imposing building still stands today but the bottom five windows have all disappeared - to be replaced by modern plate glass ones. The photograph dates from around 1920 and shows what is today Movie Mix and the NFU Mutual office in Bridgeland Street. The building also houses the meeting room of the Bideford Bridge Trust.

Friendship's Café opposite Butcher's Row in the Pannier Market has always been a difficult building to photograph given its size and the narrowness of the road it sits in. This shot shows some of the staff and their Carnival float from sometime in the 1930s. Today the building has been transformed into flats by its owner the Bridge Trust.

It is sometimes surprising how quickly some areas change. This photograph which dates from the 1930s shows, on the right, the still existing large building called Stanhope in Northam Road. The building site on the right was about to be developed as the now closed post office along with a terrace of houses.

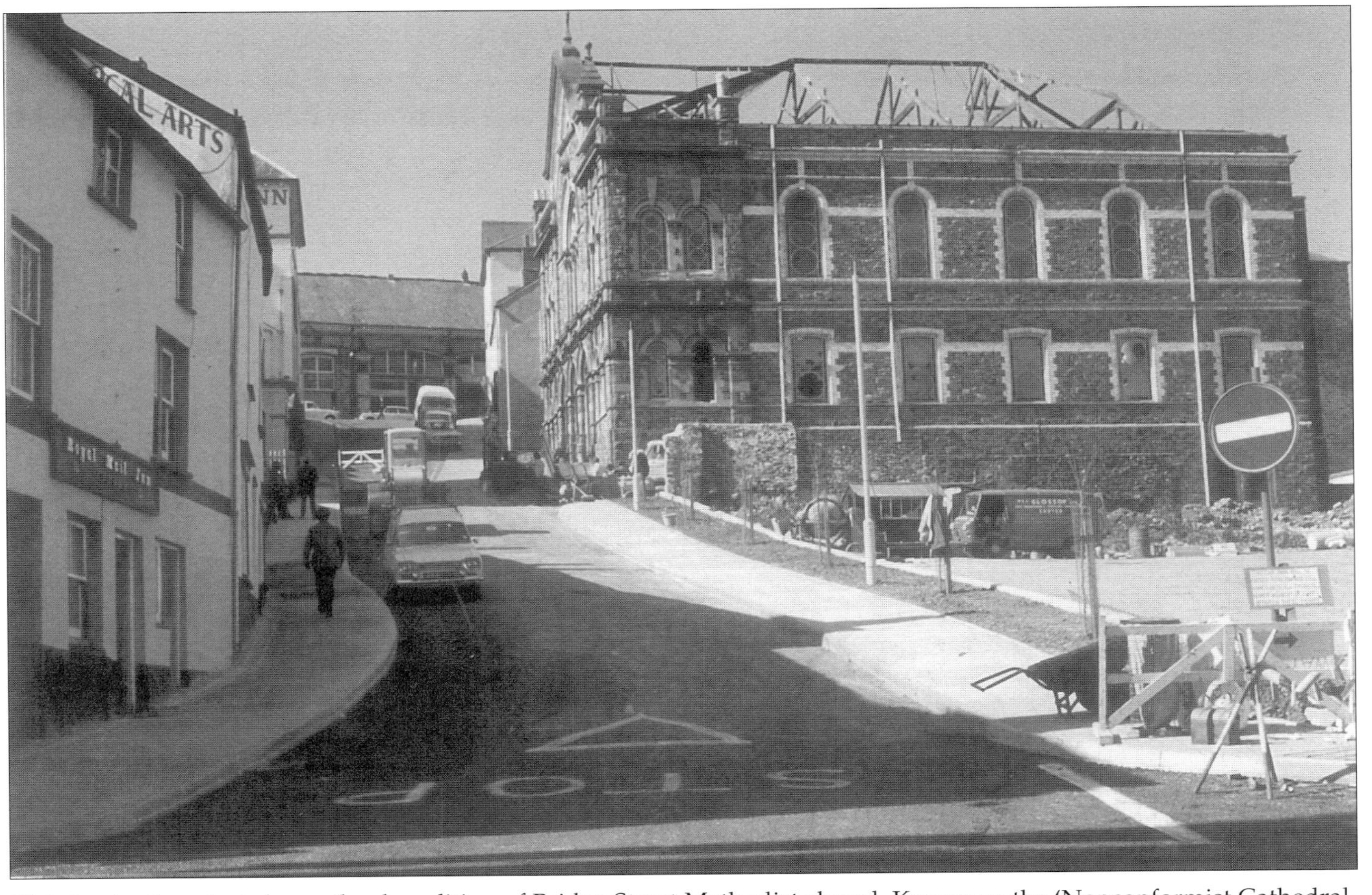

This fascinating shot shows the demolition of Bridge Street Methodist chapel. Known as the 'Nonconformist Cathedral of North Devon' its removal was very contentious and looking at it nearly 40 years or so later it does seem a pity it was ever knocked down so handsome and imposing a building was it.

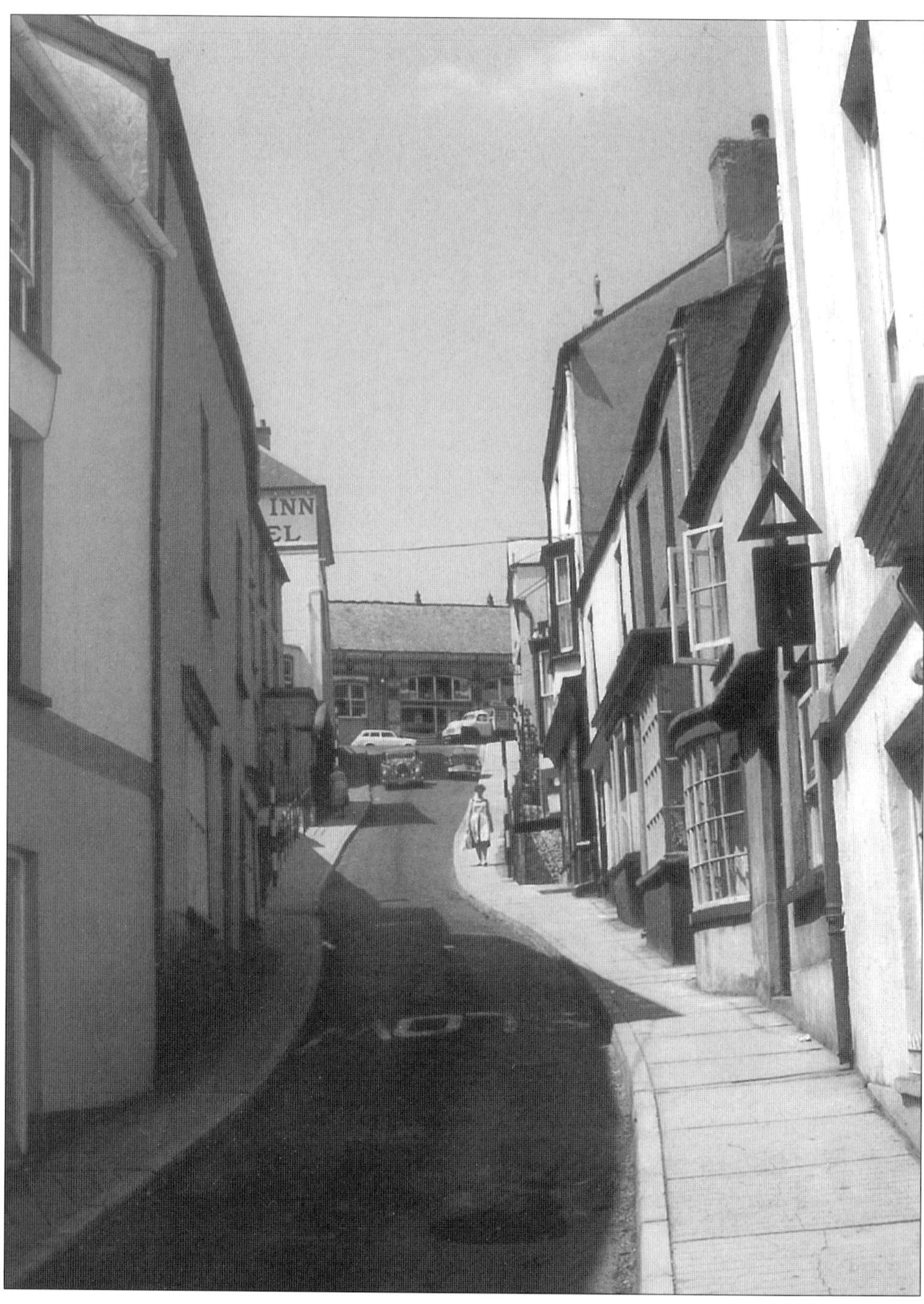

Bridge Street also housed a series of smaller buildings - shops and houses - and they are shown in this picture which was obviously taken before the previous one. The buildings went - to be replaced by a rather soul-less car park. Not a very good exchange perhaps?

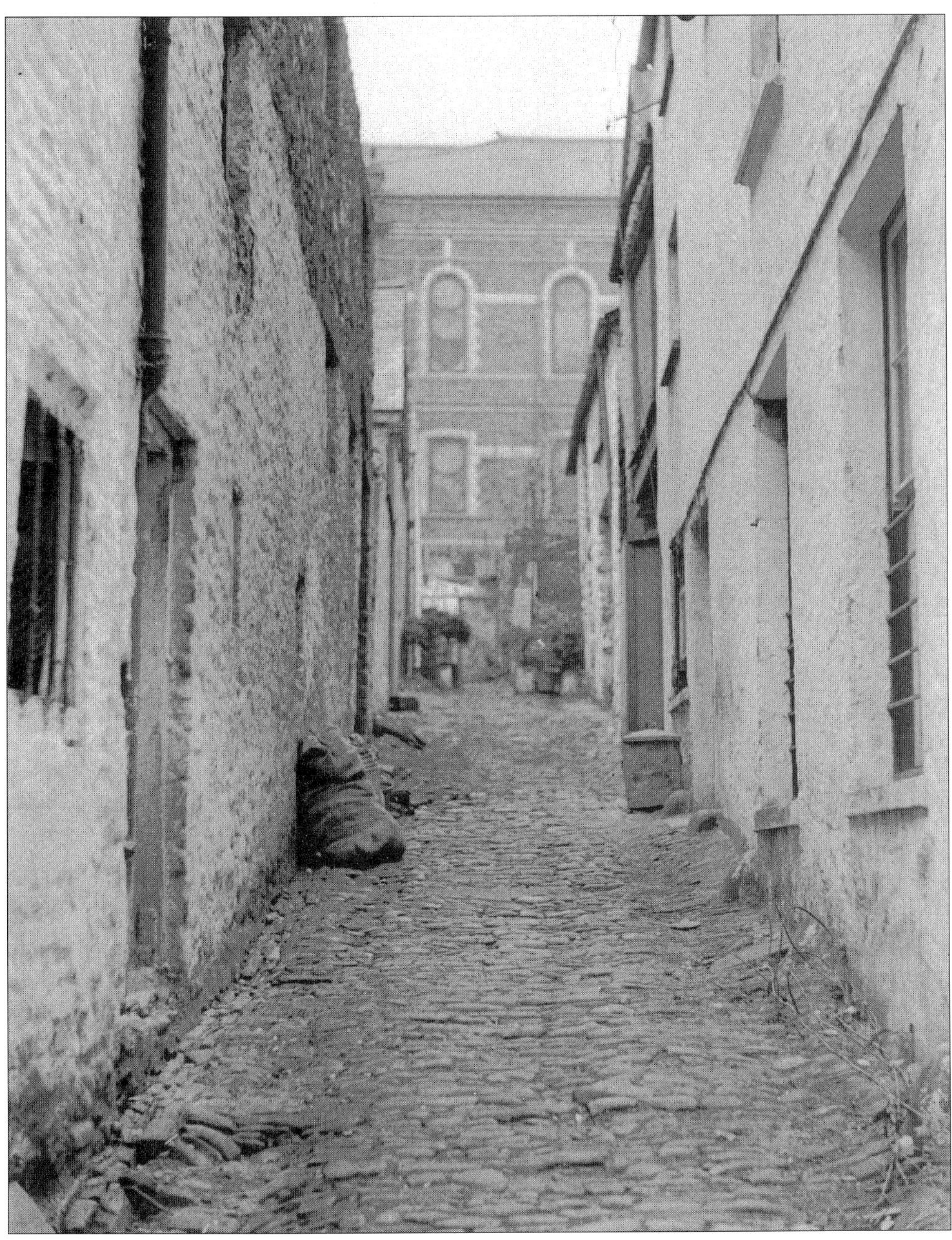

This piece of old Bideford is today a small unnamed lane between Allhalland Street and the Bridge Street car park. When this photograph was taken in 1953 the massive Wesleyan Methodist chapel was still present - but this has long gone. The cobblestones on the path are still present, albeit with a series of slate slabs down the middle. The original name of the lane was Union Street.

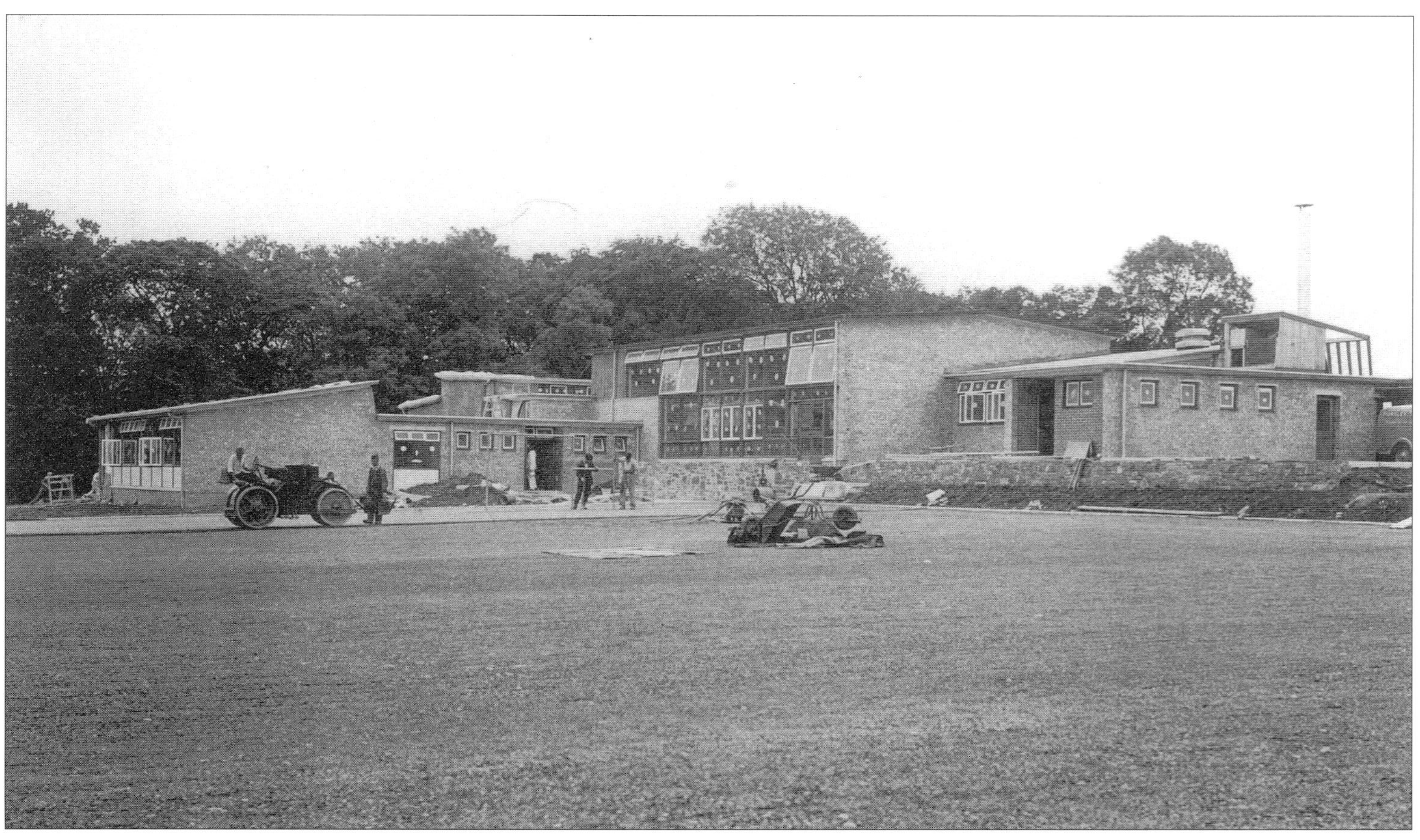

In 1958 Devon county council Education Authority built Westcroft School and this photograph shows construction coming to an end. I wonder how many Bidefordians have gone through the school over the last 50 years?

Some of these seventeenth-century cottages in North Road still survive today but others were demolished in the 1960s during so called 'slum clearances' by the borough council. They are thought to have been inhabited by people working in the old pottery kilns that were to be found in this road and in the Strand-Willet Street area just round the corner.

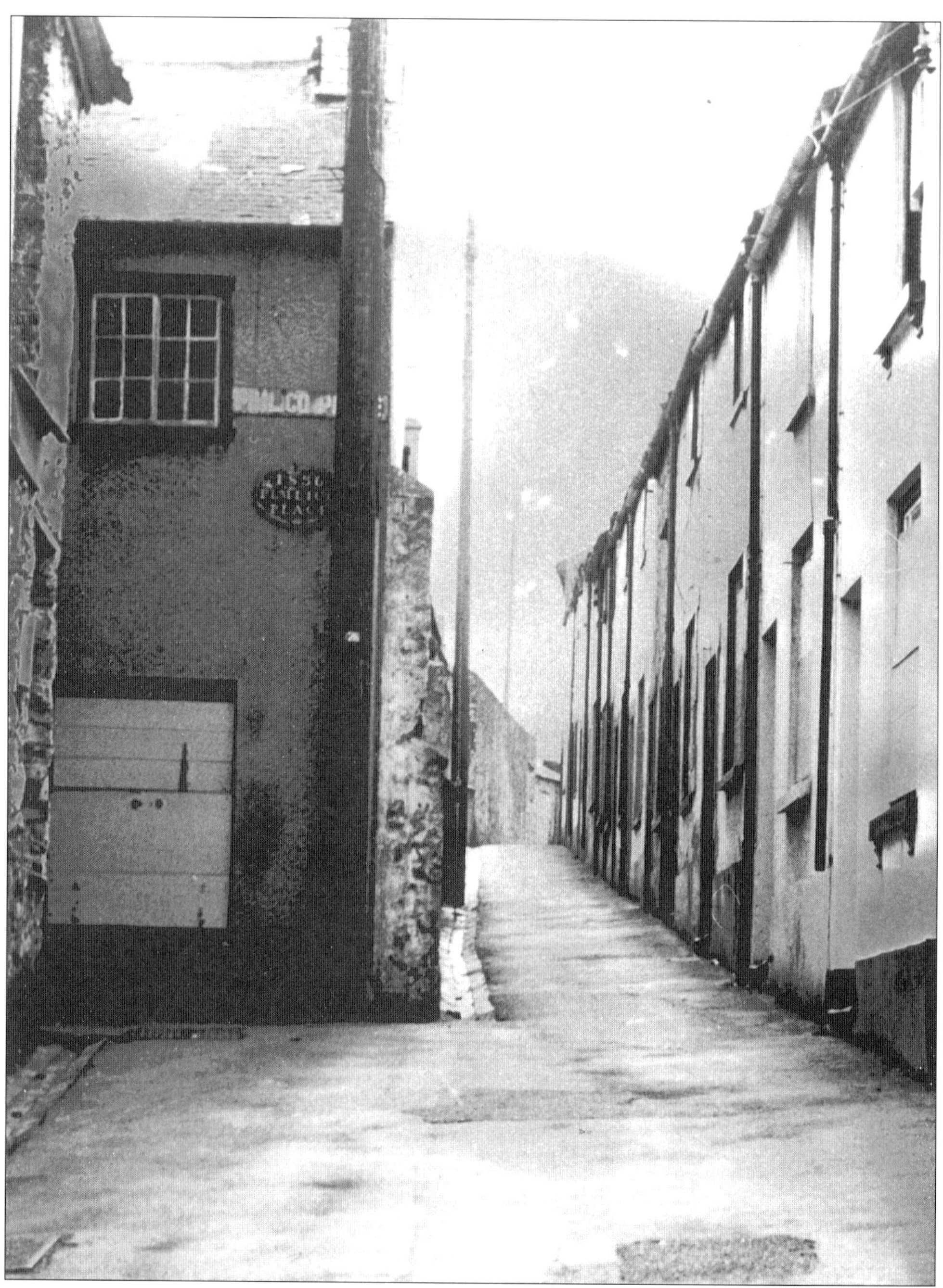

During the 1960s clearances of what the council called substandard houses saw both Pimlico Place (shown here) and Providence Place in between High Street and Honestone Street being demolished. True the houses were small but people I have talked to who lived there at different times said the area was very close-knit and friendly.

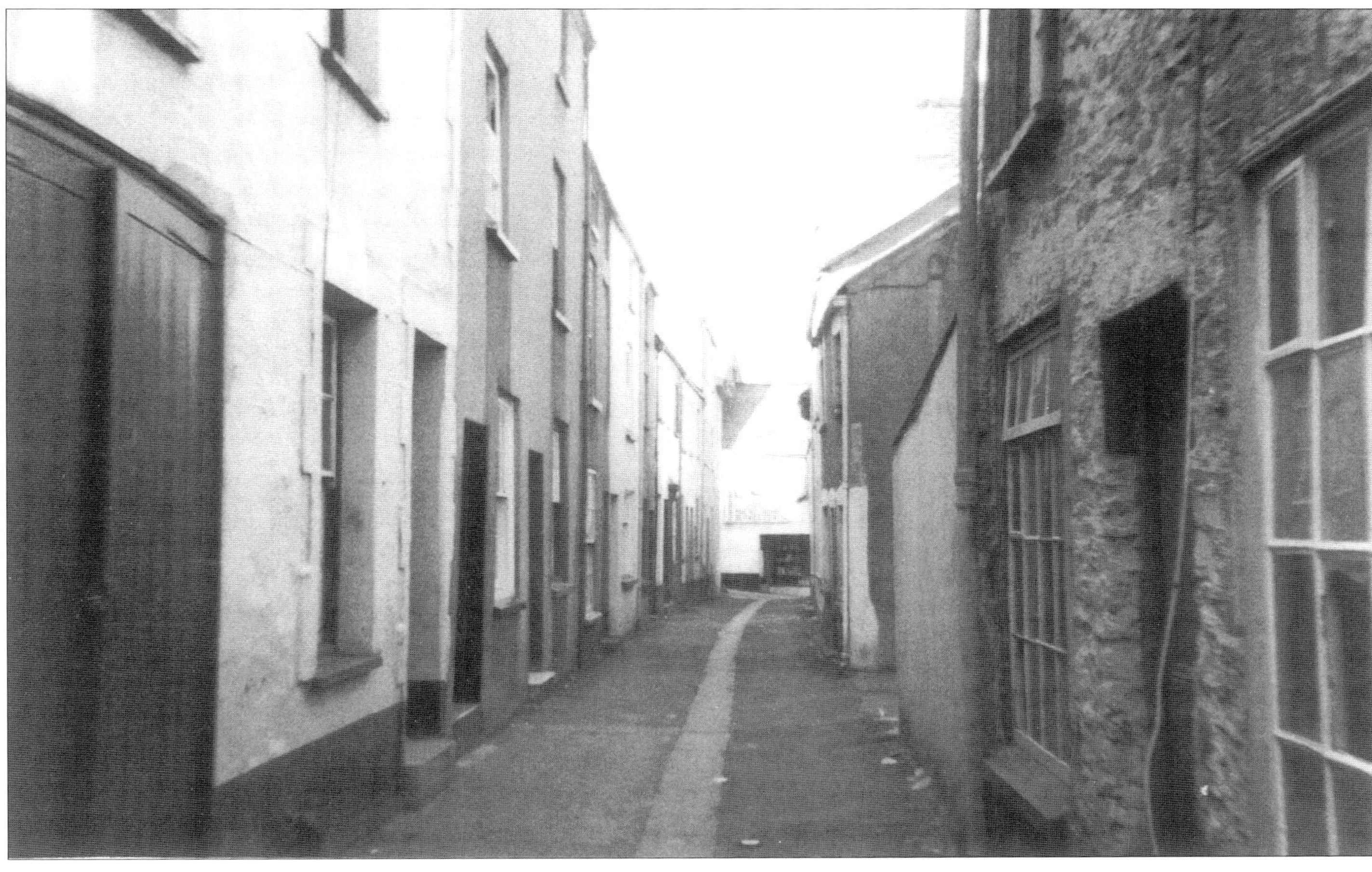

This is another part of Bideford's history which has disappeared. It shows New Street in 1971 just prior to the whole area being flattened and replaced, after quite a few years, with some new council built flats.

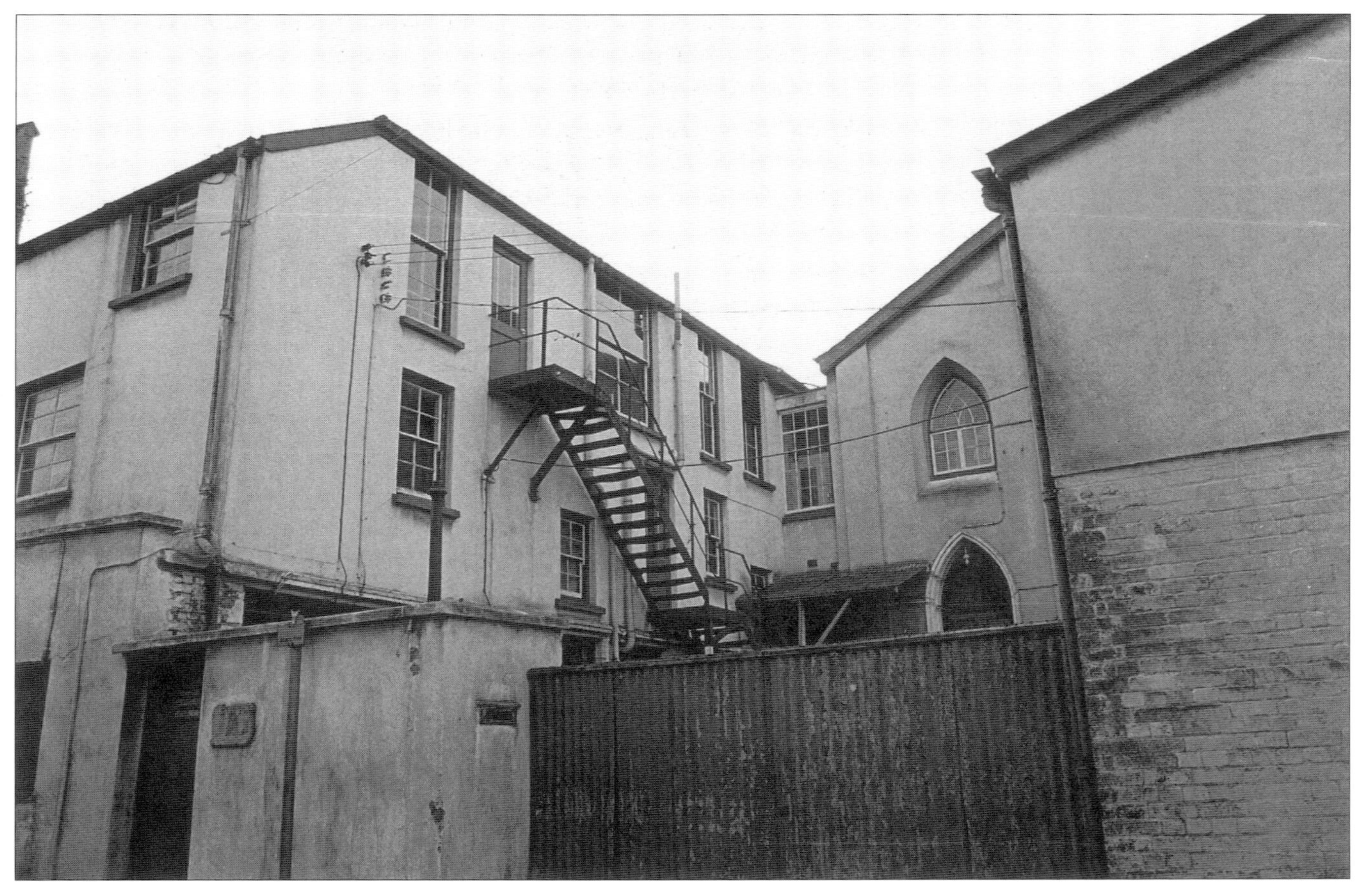

This photograph was taken in 1983 and shows the old Bible Christian chapel in Silver Street. Built in 1844 it later became a glove factory and then a snooker hall before ending its life as a fairly disreputable night club. Its chequered history finally came to a finish in 2004 when it was demolished. In this photograph the original building is almost lost among later accretions.

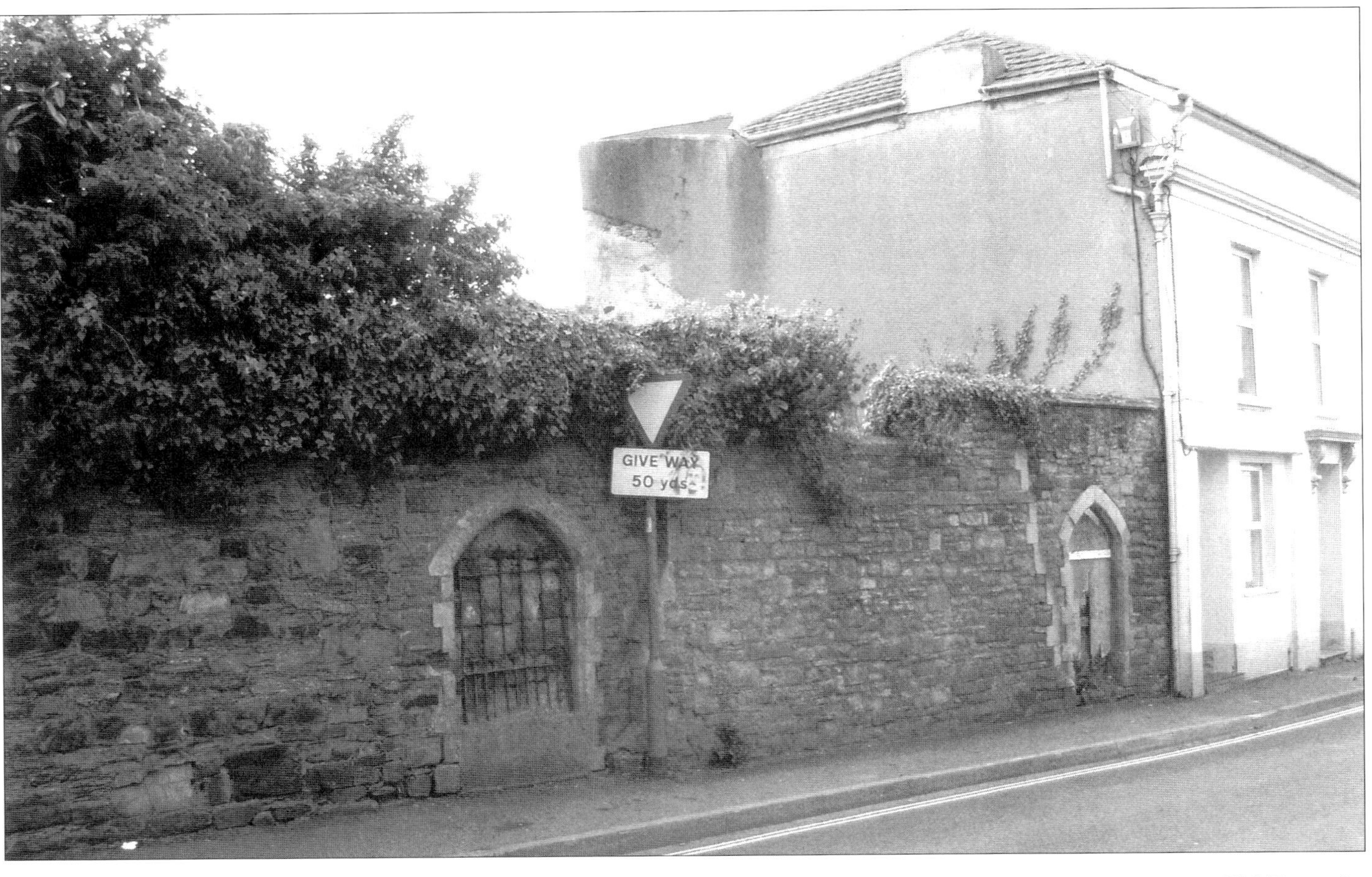

It seemed worthwhile including this photograph which shows the corner of the old borough cemetery in Old Town in June 2009. Since then the site, which once housed the cemetery caretaker's cottage, has been redeveloped by the Bridge Trust with a new house whilst the wall to the left has been lowered and refurbished by Torridge district council. The cemetery itself dates from 1841 and is notable as one of the first council run cemeteries in Britain.

Industry

In the eighteenth and nineteenth centuries many provincial towns boasted their own banks and these firms often issued their own bank notes. Bideford was no exception and this £1 note was issued in November 1813. Note how each note was individually numbered - and even signed by one of the partners Robert Hamlyn. The hole just below his printed name shows where the note was 'spiked' at the bank after being presented for cash.

Next Page: Bideford's salmon netsmen are seen here fishing just above the Bridge in 1915. The photograph was taken by Ralph Ponsonby-Watts during a trip to the town and is a really artistic composition. Such fishermen were recorded operating in the town as long ago as 1086 in the Domesday Book.

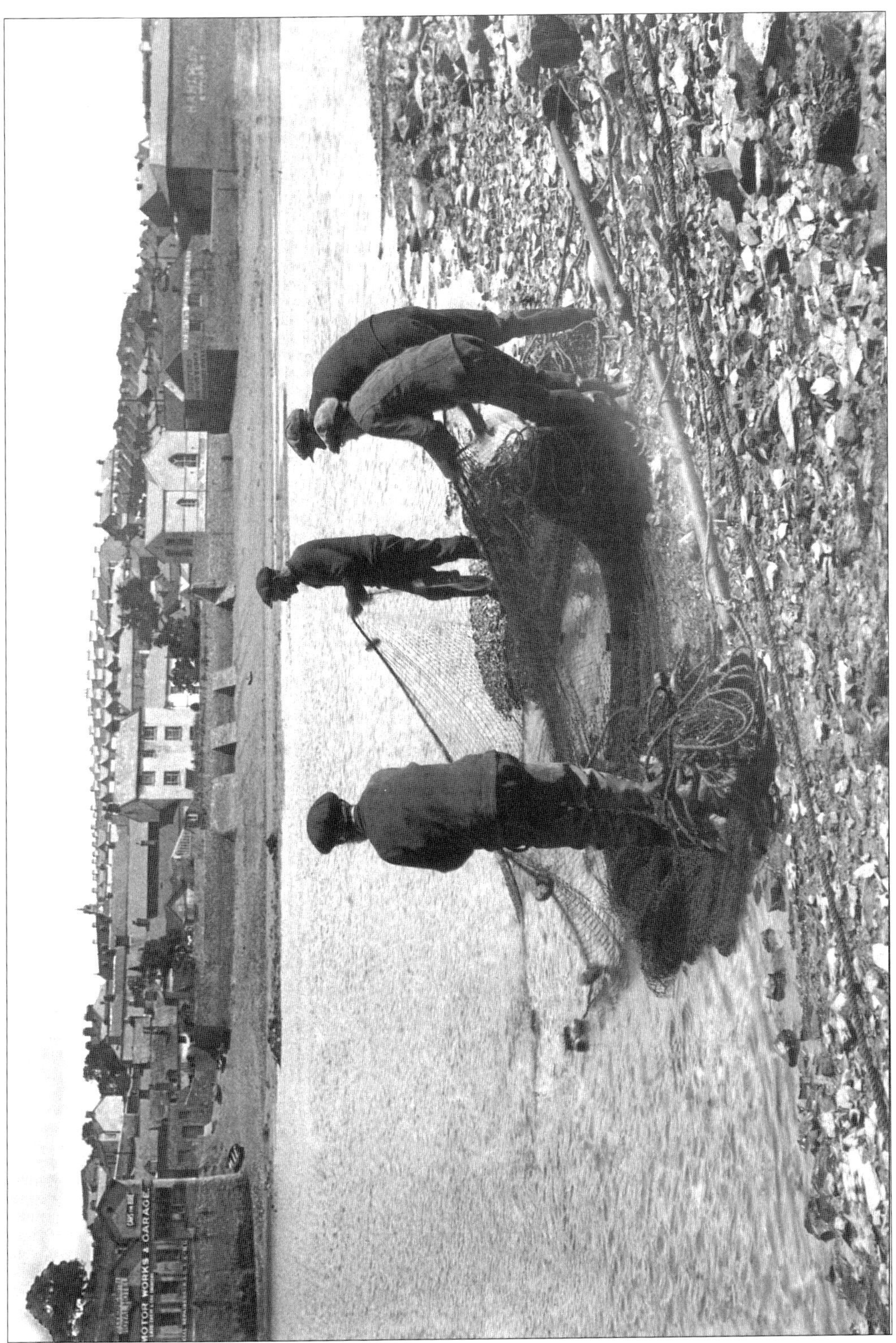
MOTOR WORKS & GARAGE

One of the long vanished old industries of Bideford is glovemaking and here we see the women workers (and male foreman) of the Sudbury Glove works in Silver Street sometime in the 1940s. On the right, fourth from the front is Phyllis Pascoe.

These were the livery stables of the Royal Hotel at East-the-Water photographed in the early 1970s. Such buildings were vital when most road transport was still horse driven but as motor cars took over so many of these old buildings became garages. These buildings can be seen on the left of the 1915 photograph on page 67.

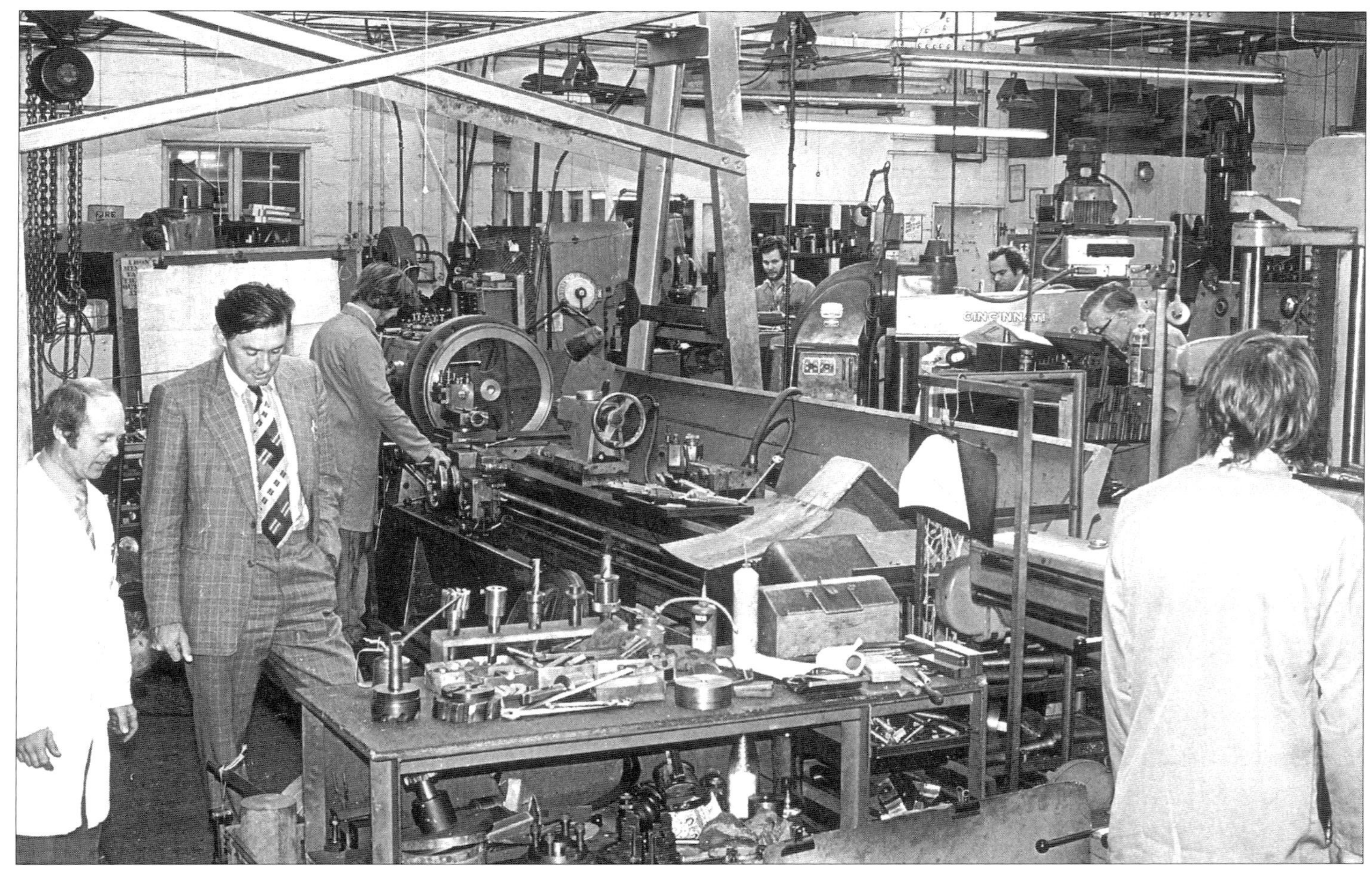

Photographs showing the interiors of working factories are not that common in my experience so these particular ones are very welcome. They show the Whiteland Engineering works at Bideford in September 1980. The firm began in war-time Nissen huts in Torrington Lane at East-the-Water in 1956 and over the years expanded to the then new factory seen here.

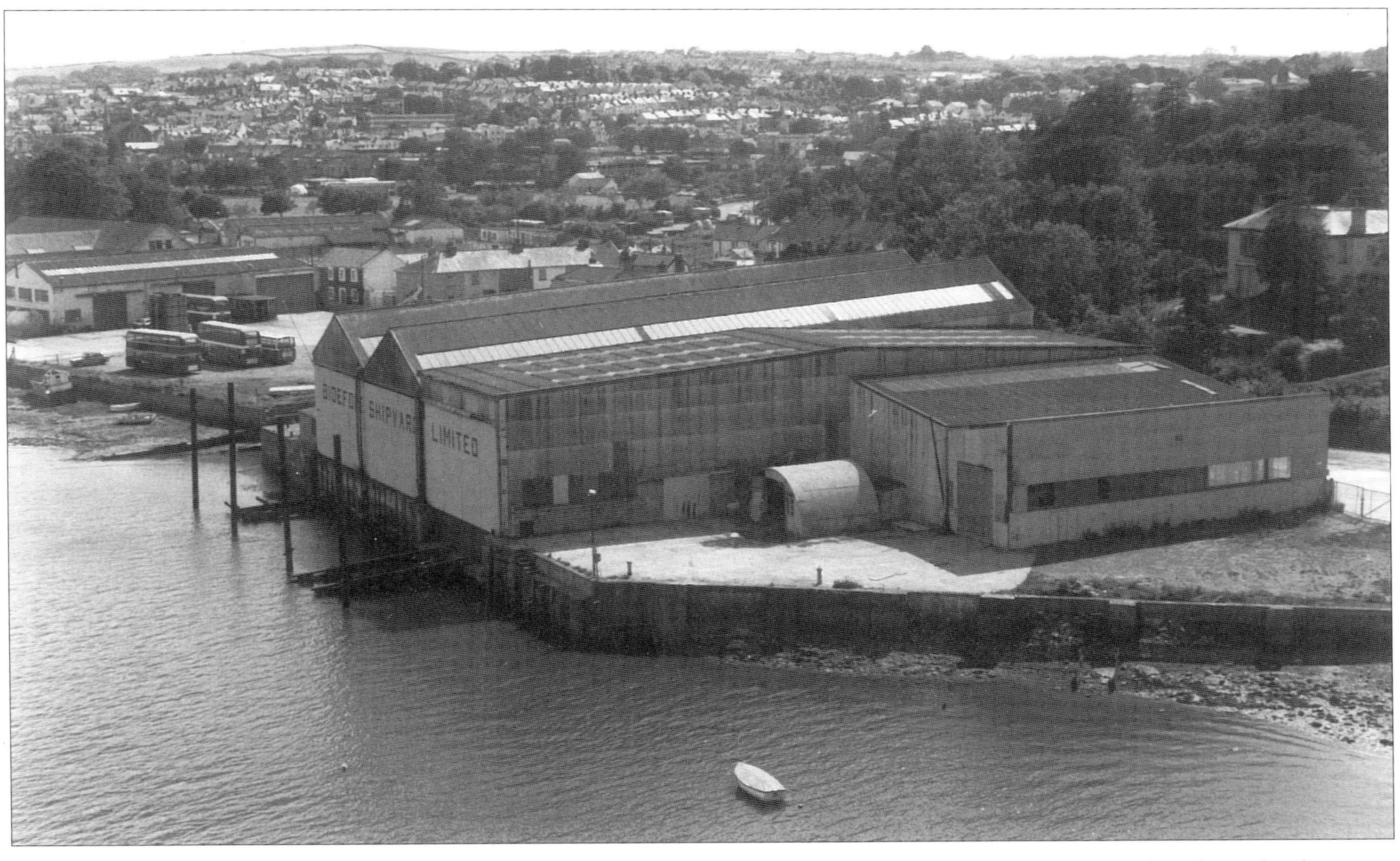

The premises of the old Bideford Shipyard with the bus depot behind it are shown well in the picture taken from the then new Torridge Bridge around 1987. The yard was developed in 1921 by Sven Hansen who built steel steamships there until 1924 when he closed it although it was later re-opened by Grimston-Aster Ltd. who themselves were replaced by Bideford Shipyard Ltd. in 1964 before being finally closed in 1983.

Transport

This shows the first Bidefordian owned car in 1902. It was a belt-driven 4 fi hp Benz which had been purchased by Dr.E.J.Toye. The driver is W.Jewell who joined the 1st Devons in World War One and was killed in 1915. Dr.Toye went on to become a much loved Mayor of Bideford.

Opposite page : The Bideford Cycling Club pictured on a club run sometime before the First World War. The coming of relatively cheap bicycles revolutionised transport for many allowing, for the first time, the freedom to travel on one's own through the villages and lanes of North Devon and England.

This Bideford based horse-drawn charabanc was photographed outside the Hoops Inn on a day excursion around 1910. The solid wheels and hard stone-based roads cannot have given a smooth or overly comfortable ride - but the customers certainly got a lot of fresh air.

"Moworks" Bideford.
One of the "Bideford Motor Works" Hire Cars.
Phone No. 45.

This photograph wasn't taken in Bideford but does show one of the hire cars on offer from Bideford Motor Works around 1910-14. If you wished to buy a car at this time the same outlet was offering a 5-seat Ford car for £170 - a very large sum at this date.

This is a marvellously detailed photograph of the long vanished Bideford, Westward Ho! And Appledore Railway on the Quay. The likewise vanished building to the left of Kingsley's Statue was the old 'Manor House'. The shot would seem to date from around 1910 and was mounted on a card stamped 'Daily Mirror Copyright London.'

When the Bideford and Westward Ho! railway (the Appledore link was added later) was built over the years 1898-1901 Bideford town council tried to stop construction and the railway company forcibly and unexpectedly laid down the line against the council's wishes. A famous and much reprinted series of photographs recorded this event but here is one that has never been published before - a real slice of 'history in the making'.

Overleaf: The Bideford, Westward Ho! and Appledore railway has featured in many books but I do not recall ever seeing this photograph before. It shows one of the two engines, probably at Westward Ho!, decorated with evergreen branches and flags plus a picture of George V on the front below the chimney. It was taken in 1911 when the railway company marked the king's coronation of that year. The tall gentleman second from left is Bidefordian Frederick Palmer who was the engine's fireman. Unfortunately he was badly injured during the First World War and never wholly recovered.

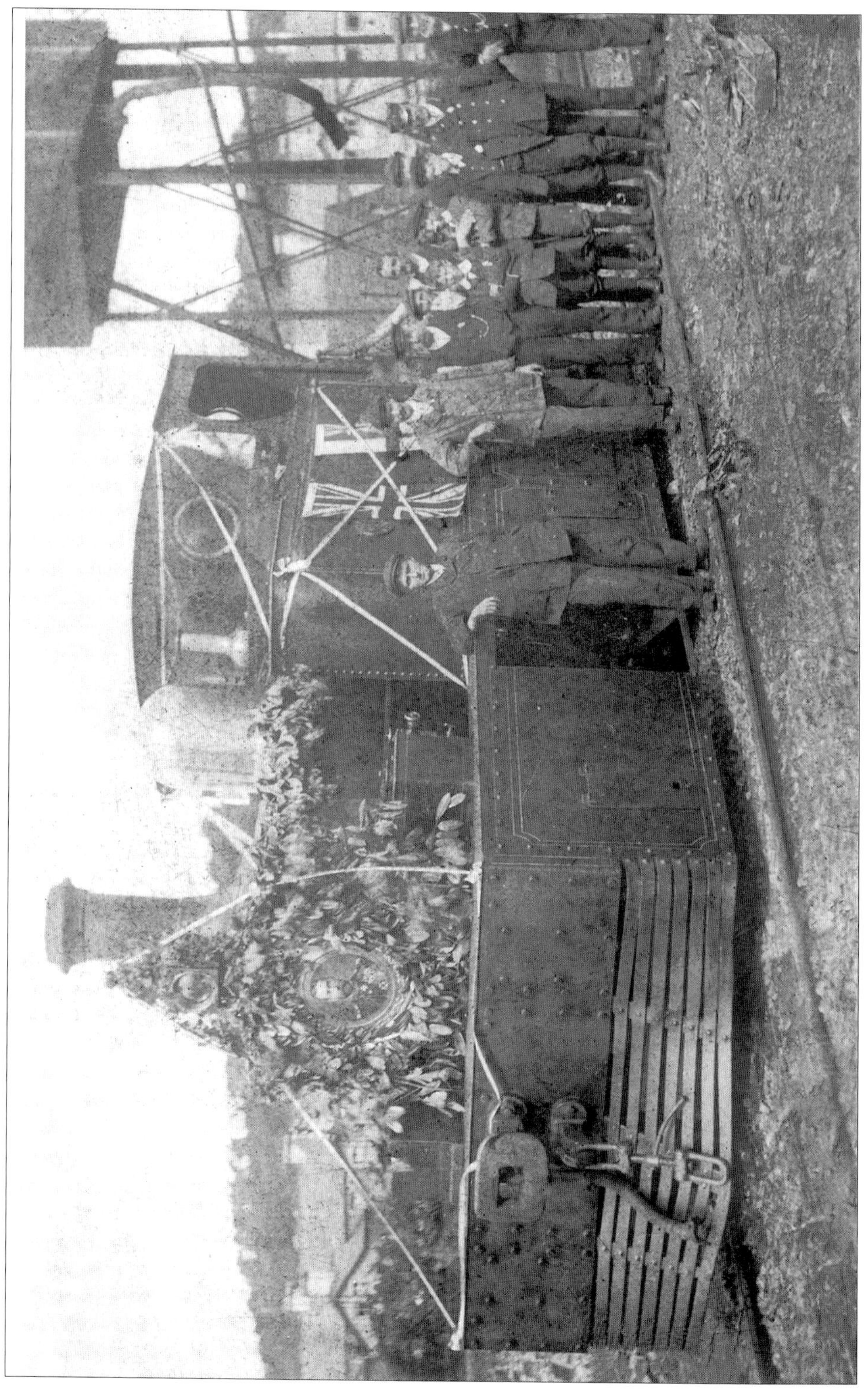

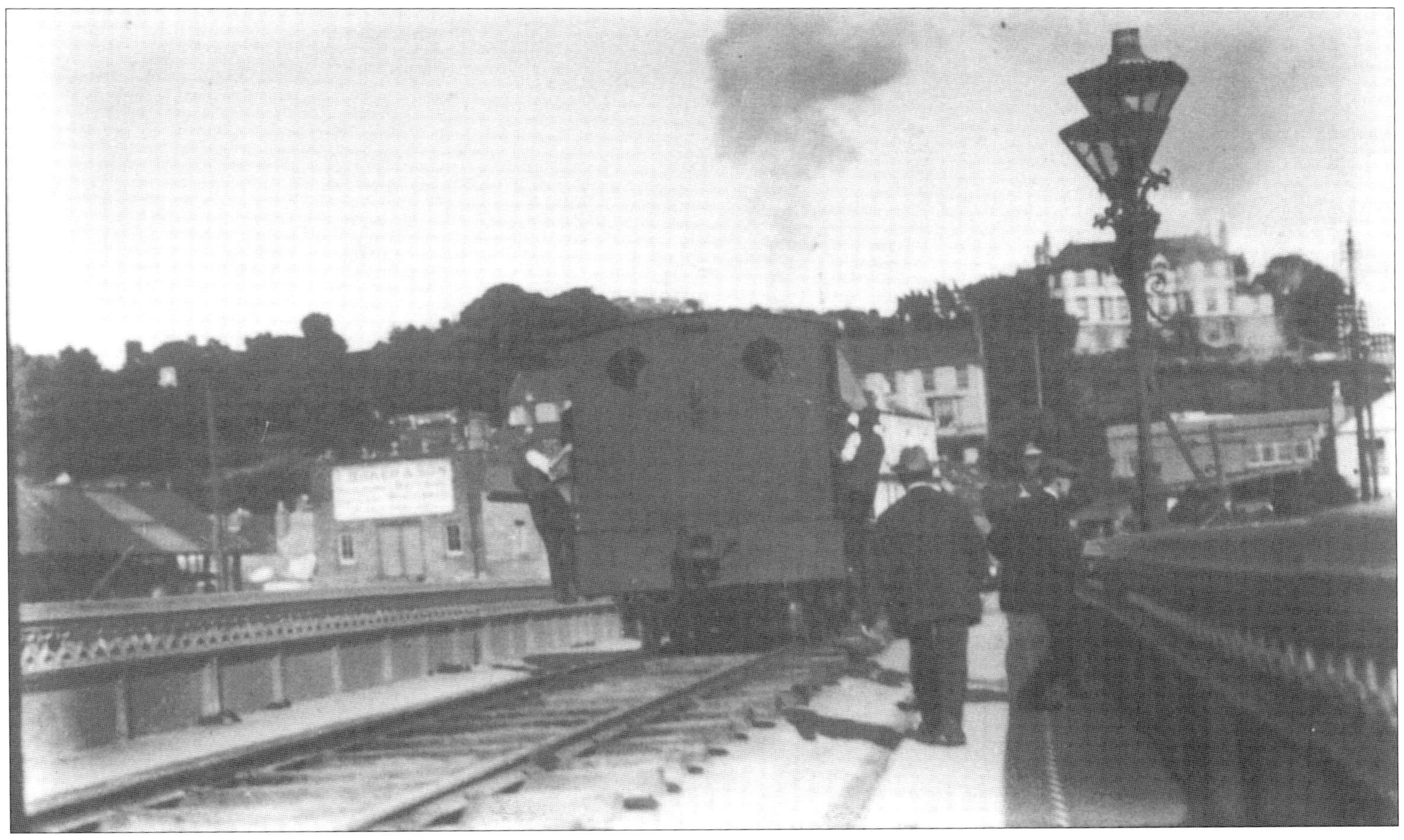

In July 1917 the engines of the Bideford, Westward Ho! and Appledore railway were taken across the Bridge on specially laid rails on the first part of their journey to oblivion. No-one is quite clear where they went but this shot shows one of them making its way across the Bridge.

This rather faded photograph links with the one on page 26 as it shows one of Blackmore's lorries in the early 1920s. Carbide lamps, solid tyres and an absence of side windows point to a date at the start of that decade rather than at the end - little did the people then realise that what was a novelty to them would lead to the clogged roads we experience today!

On p.71 is shown the Bideford Shipyard at Bank End and reference is made there to the firm's precursor Hansen's Shipyard. This group consists of men who worked at the yard and this dates from sometime between 1921 and 1924. I assume the men on the left were the office staff with the manual workers being distinguished by their flat caps. The lorry has no glass windows - but it does have curtains!

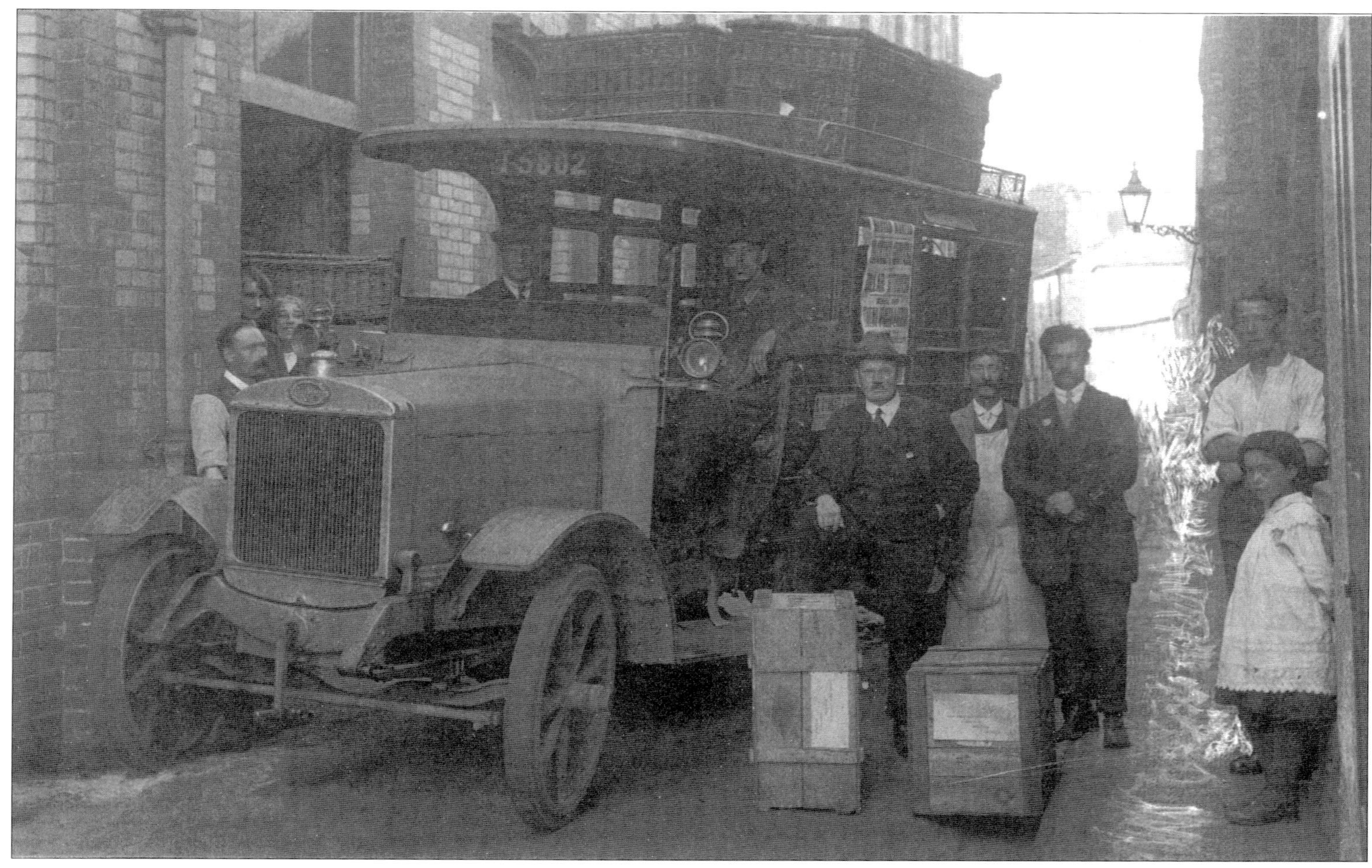

This splendid looking lorry was photographed in Rope Walk in the 1920s outside what later became the Repository and seems to have been taken to record the inauguration of a new freight service in the town.

William Pascoe poses in his chauffeur's white coat by his hire vehicle in this 1920s photograph taken in Bideford. Note his highly polished shoes which match the sheen on his vehicle. The 'TT' number plate indicates that this vehicle was registered in Devon.

Next page: This wonderful motorcycle combination was pictured outside Trick's Garage in Meddon Street in the early 1930s. These tiny 'front room' garages were the norm in the past and though small they were advertising 'Tyres, Accessories & Petrol.' The man on the motorcycle was Sid Trick and next to him are stood Charles and Bill Trick.

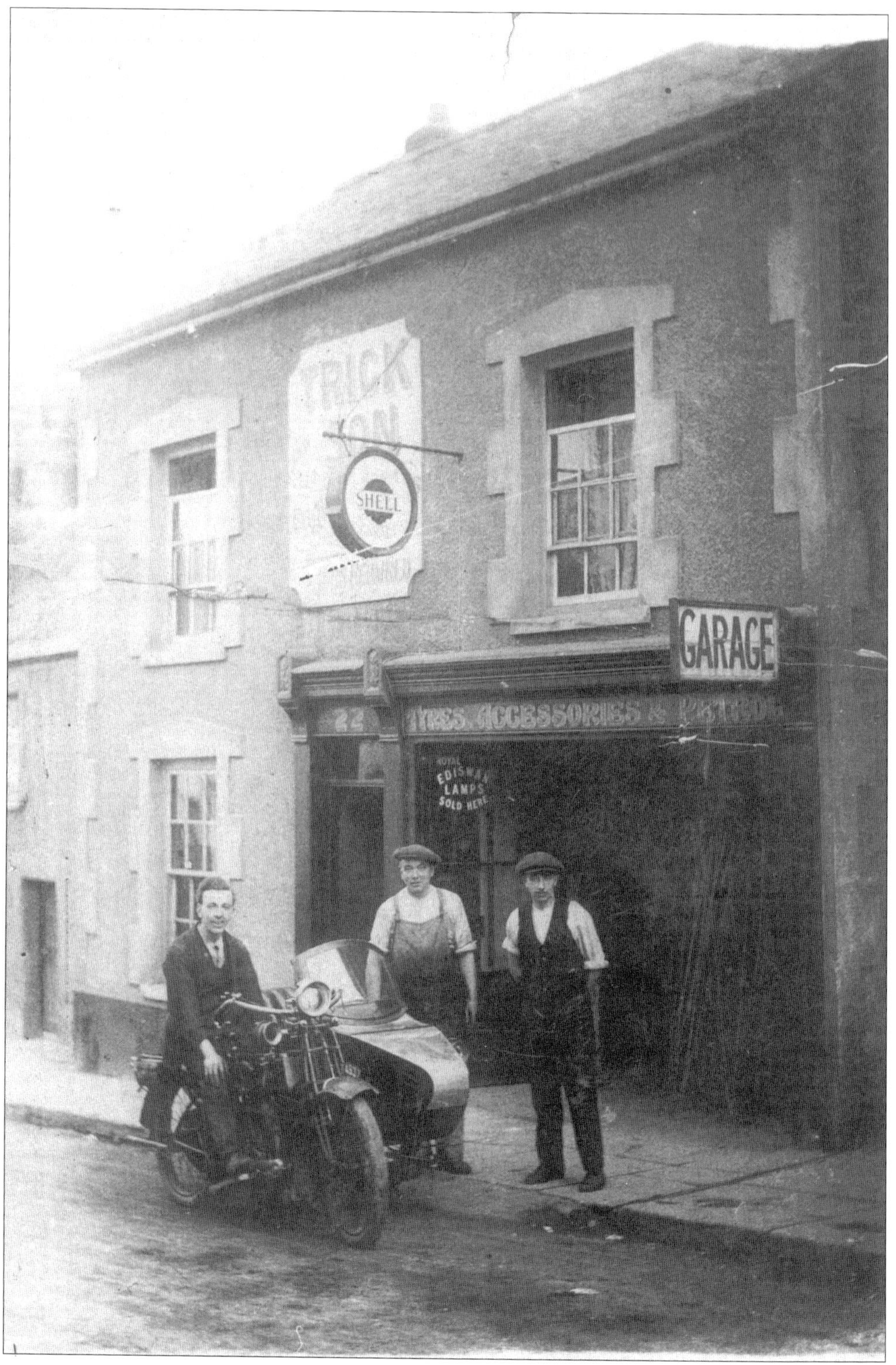
SHELL
GARAGE
22
ACCESSORIES &
ROYAL
EDISWAN
LAMPS
SOLD HERE

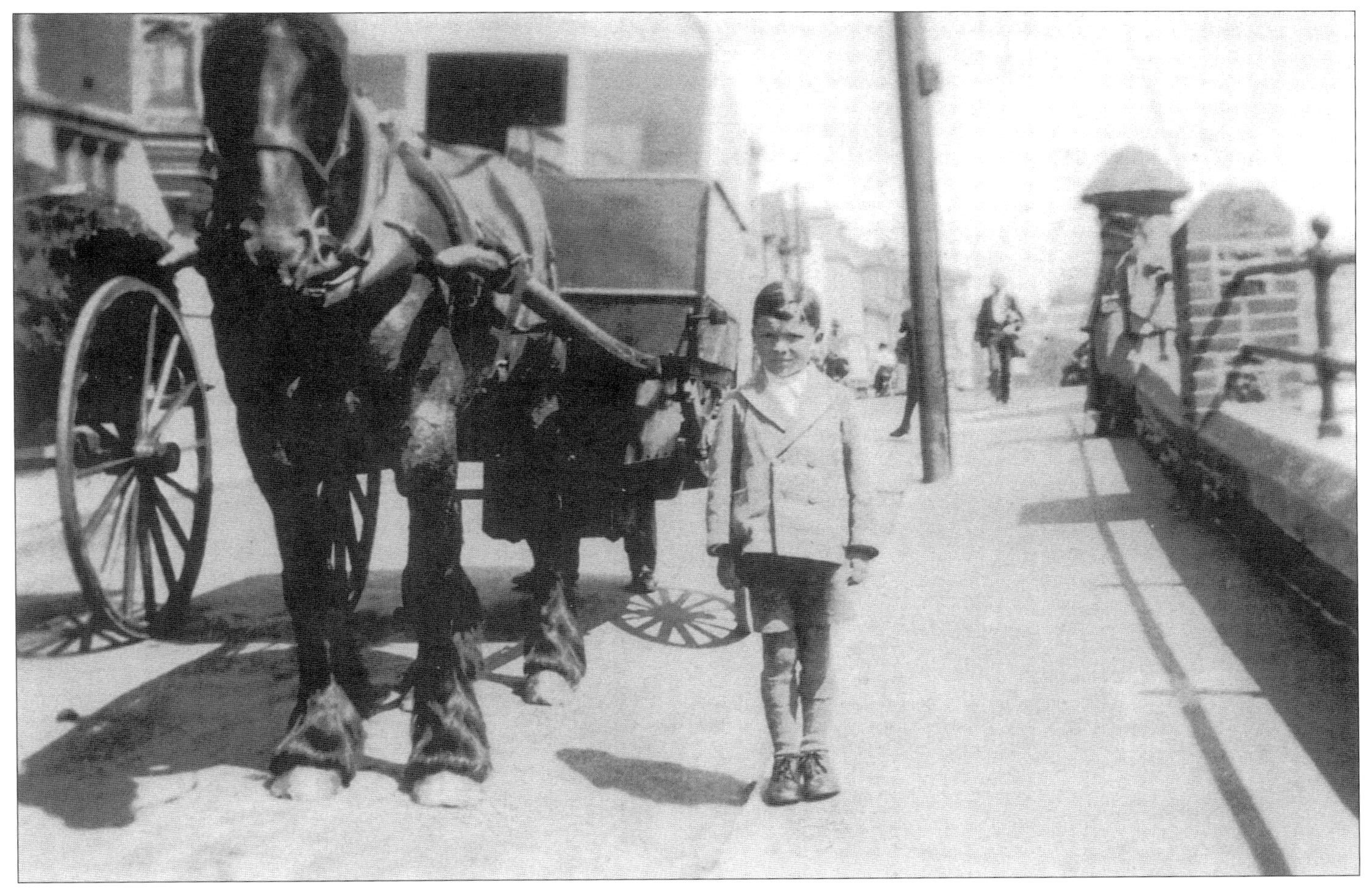

This little boy in what is evidently his 'Sunday best' is Master D.Beer standing beside his family's milk delivery cart at the western end of the Bridge sometime around 1920 - note the Library building just appearing in the top left hand corner. Beer's dairy was a large undertaking at this period with many people taking their products.

The Bridge is instantly recognisable here but what are the ships doing clogging up the river channel? This photograph shows the Torridge around 1933, a period when some 30 under-employed cargo vessels were laid up in the 'free' anchorage provided by the river - many of which didn't disappear until the late 1930s. The wooden walkways out to them were for many years obvious at low tide alongside the 'Westleigh straight' but have now all virtually disappeared.

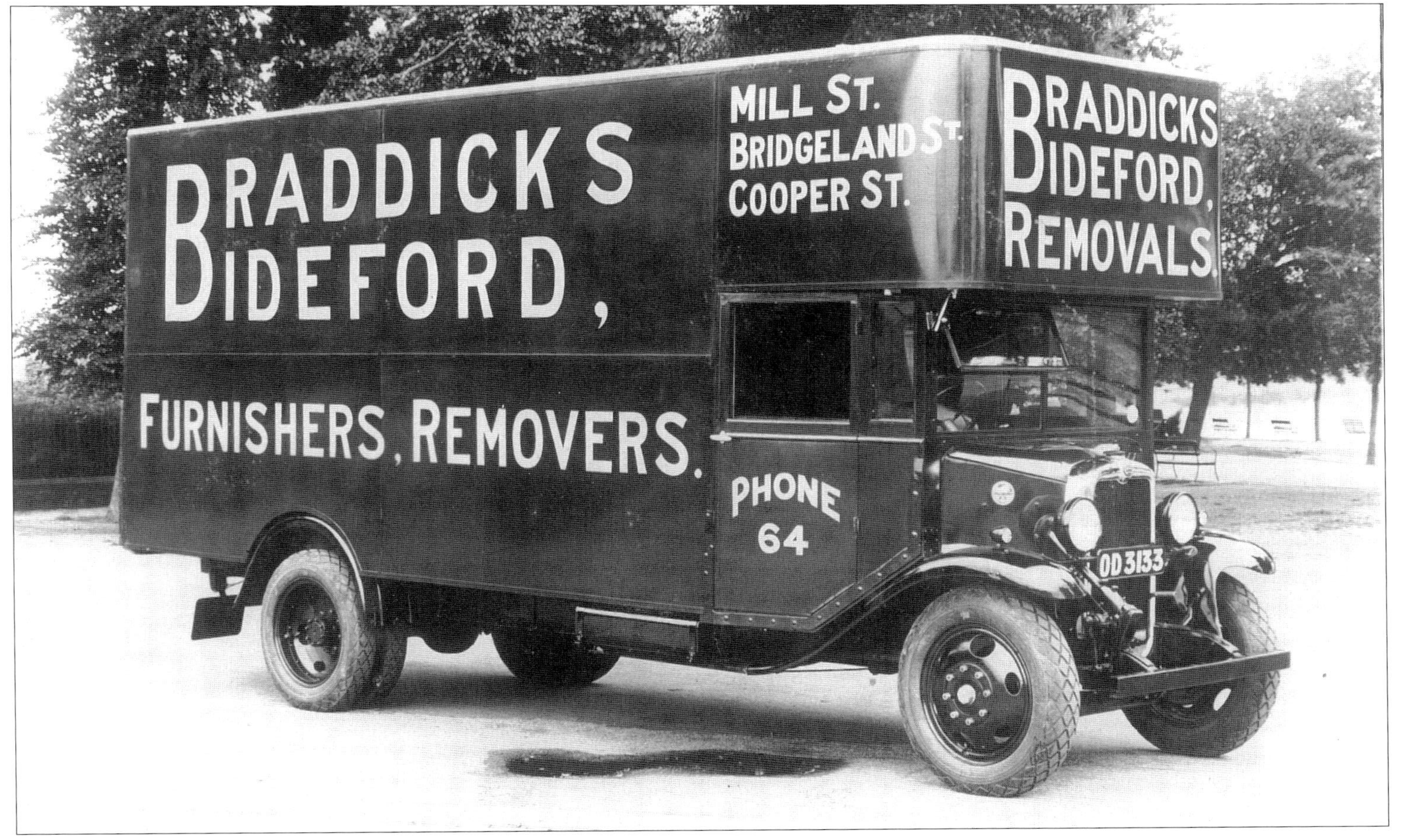

What a wonderful looking vehicle this is! In Volume 2 I published a shot of a fairly basic looking lorry owned by Braddick's in the 1920s and compared with this one the driver must have been overcome by the luxury - pneumatic tyres, glass windows and electric lights. Some old features are still present - the 'split' front window and absence of windscreen wipers. What might also strike us today is the small size of this removal van in comparison to today's huge pantechnicons - but there again everyone owned less in the past.

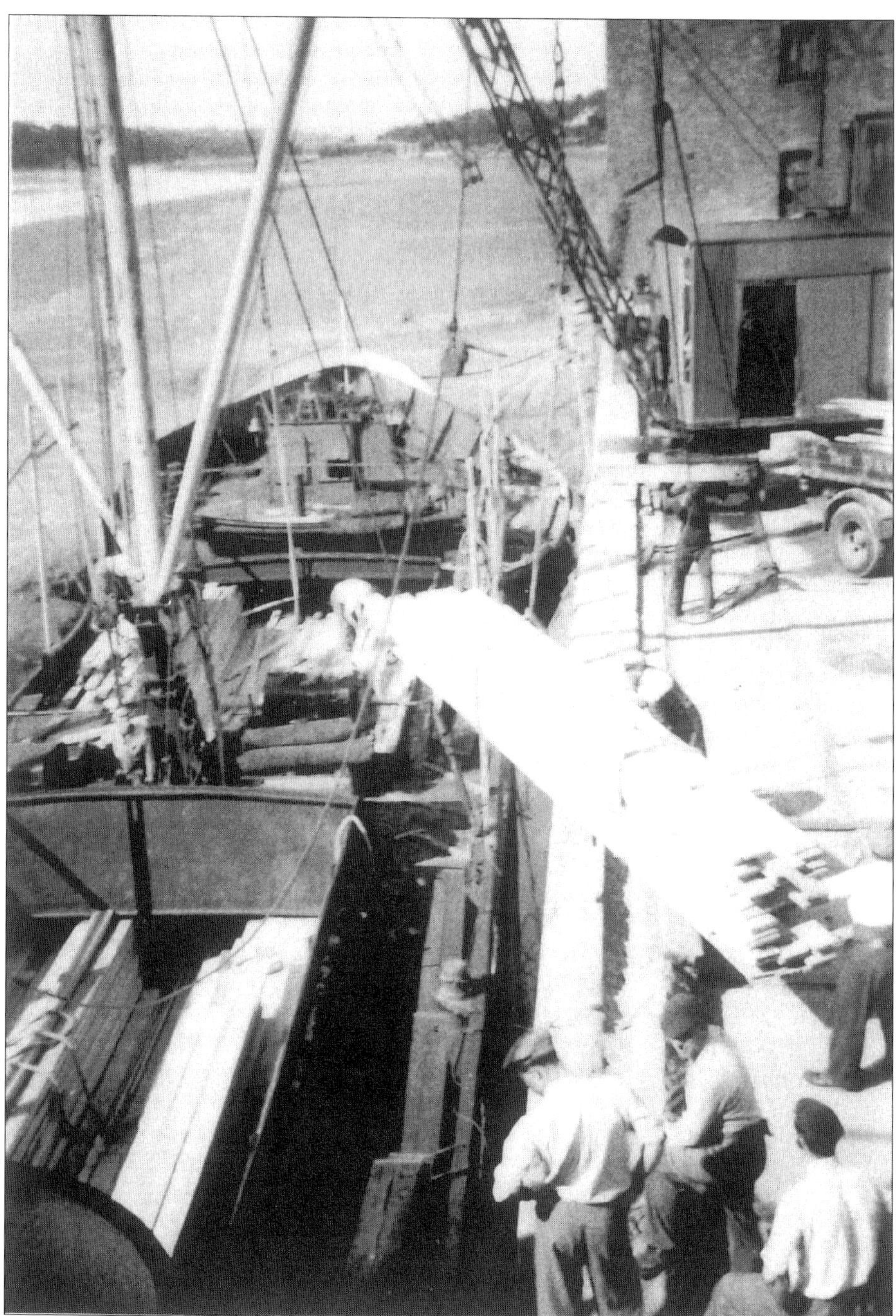

This is a close-up of a mobile crane taken in the 1950s when timber was being discharged from a vessel alongside Clarence Wharf - it isn't very probable that we will ever see a scene like this again but given the increasing problems with roads one never knows.

The 'Devonia' steamship was long associated with Bideford carrying both passengers and cargo up to Bristol and other local ports. This fine shot shows the vessel getting up steam as it leaves Bideford.

Overleaf: The small scale of both vessels and lorries in the 1950s is captured well in this picture showing planking being unloaded on Bideford Quay. Compare this view to the highly mobile and massive crane used today - and the large lorries that bring ball clay to the port.

Bartlett's

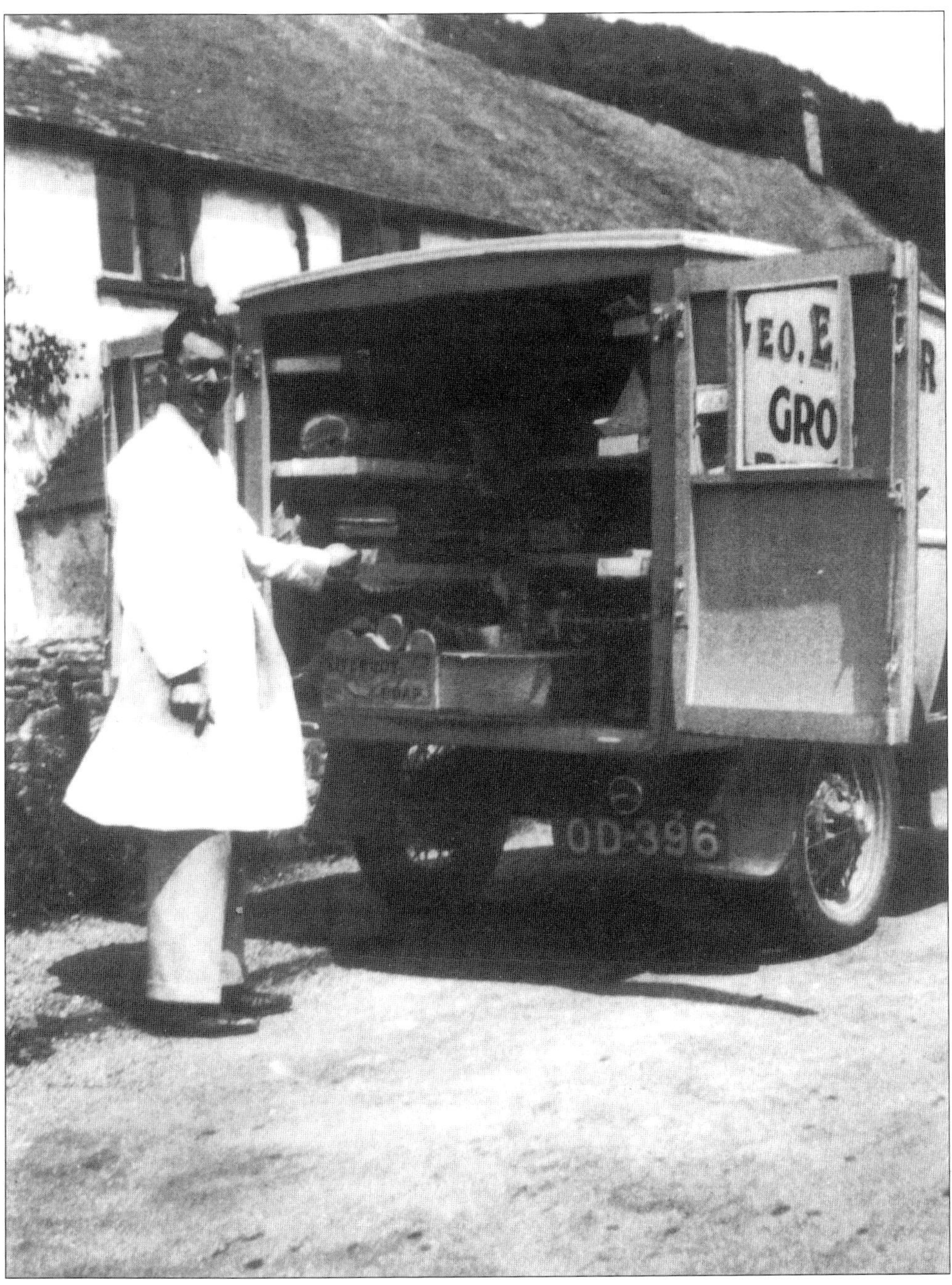

The ubiquity of small home-delivery vehicles run by today's supermarkets is nothing new. In the past a wide range of foodstuffs was delivered and also sold from travelling dealers. Here from the 1950s we see Bideford-based George Beer's grocery van on a village call.

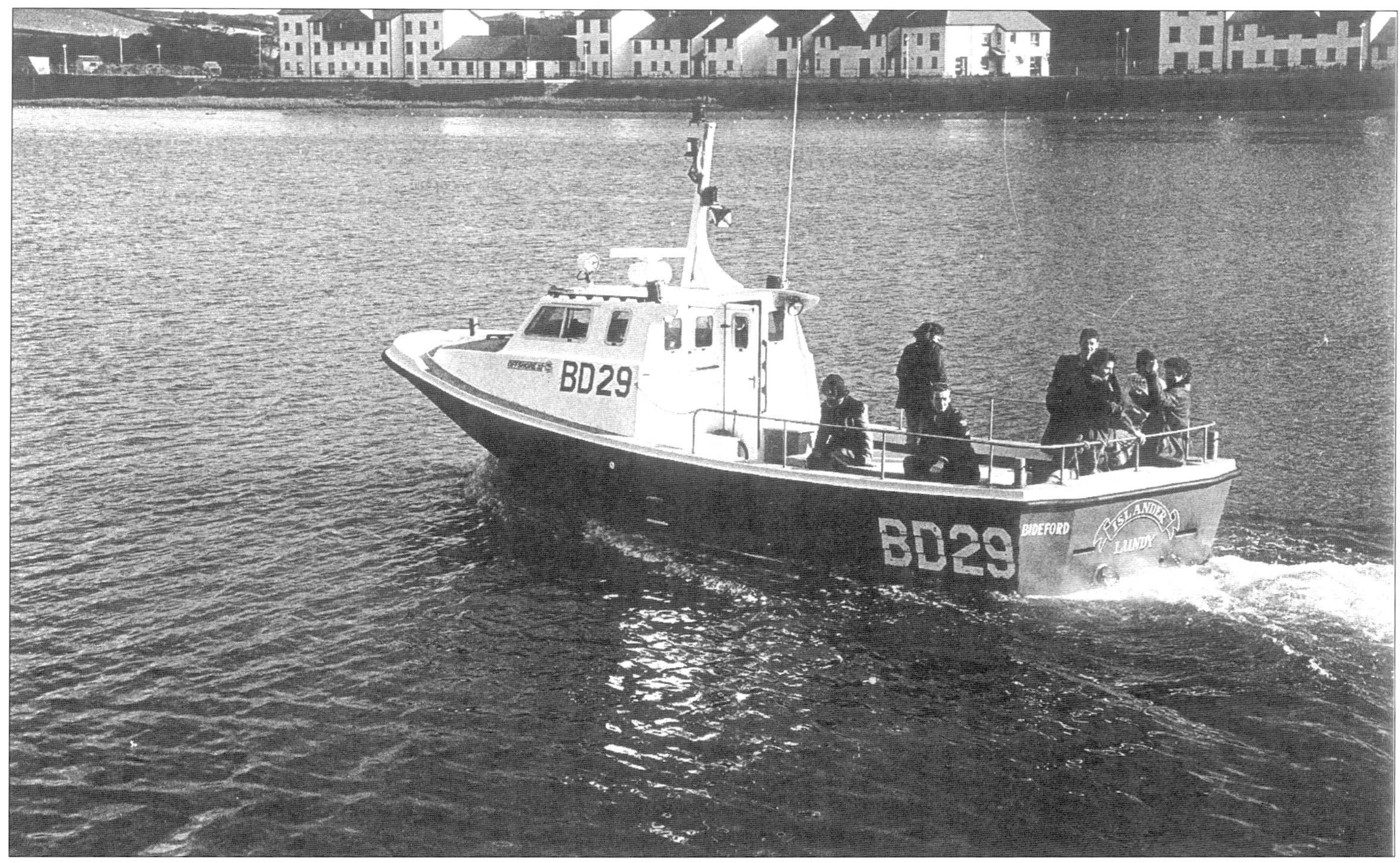

Lundy islanders have relied on many different vessels over the years for their links to the mainland and this photograph, from November 1985, shows the 'Islander' a very small, though wonderfully streamlined, vessel which was operating on the Lundy run at this date.

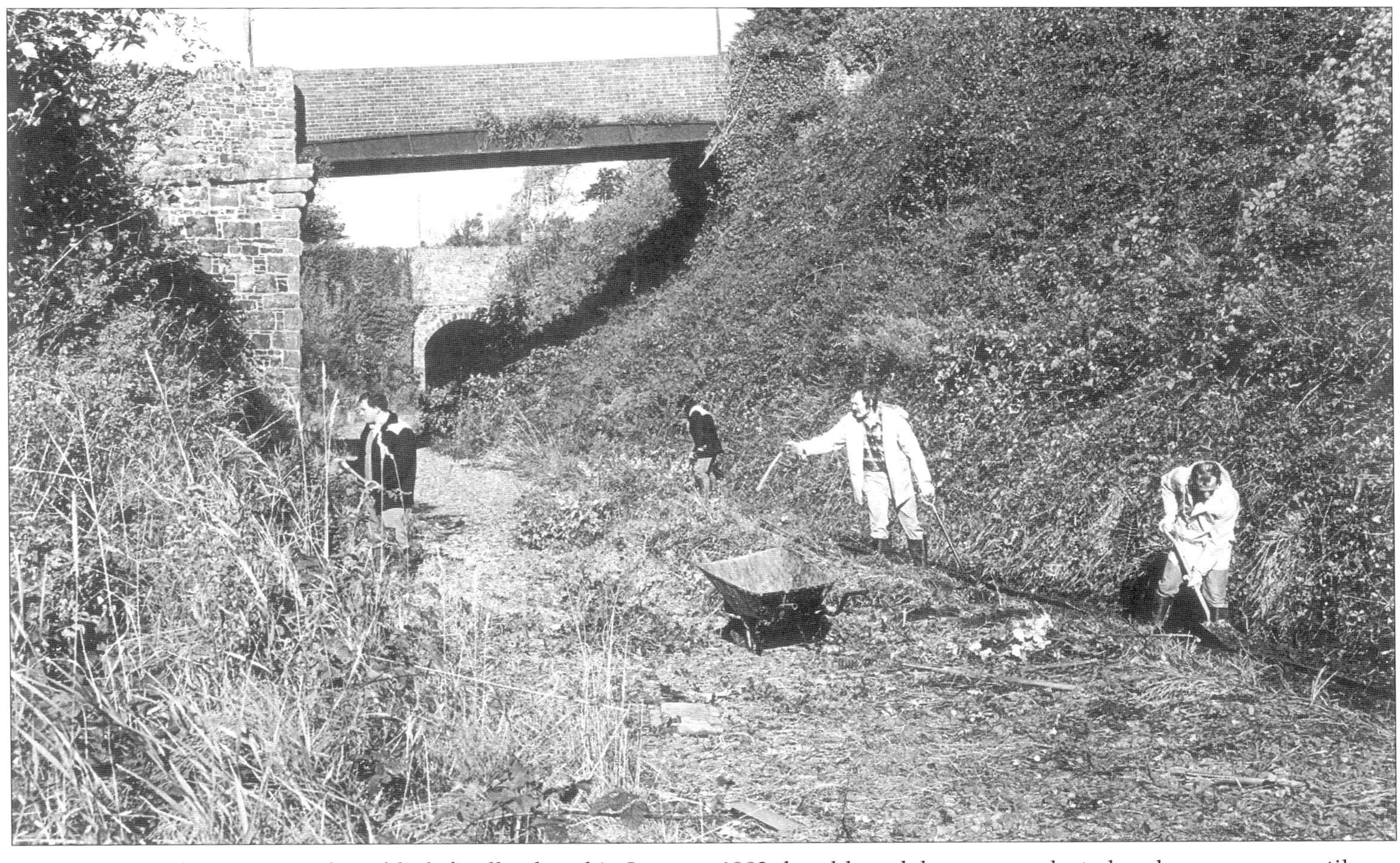

When the Bideford-Barnstaple rail link finally closed in January 1983 the old track became neglected and overgrown until November 1985 when work began to clear the line and re-open it as the Tarka Trail which has, of course, become enormously popular with walkers and cyclists. This photograph shows the initial clearance work beginning in 1985.

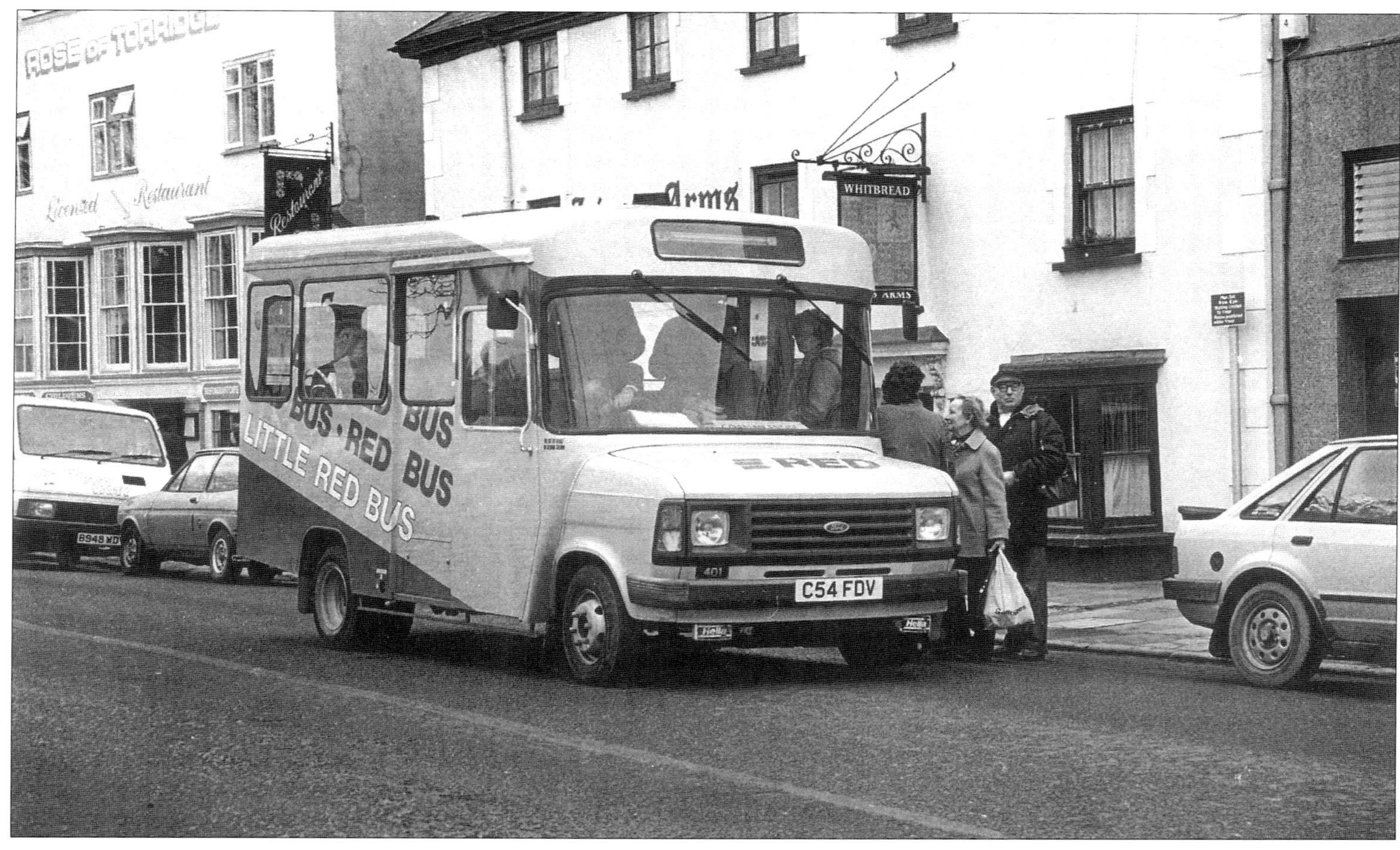

In January 1986 the local bus company introduced their 'Little Red Minibus' service. The idea of these new buses was that they could be hailed anywhere along their routes rather like a taxi. The system soon disappeared but at least we have this photograph of the first service outside the Kings Arms on the Quay in that month - with the Rose of Torridge café in the background.

This fine shot of the Lundy supply vessel the m.v. *Oldenburg* dates from 1986. The quayside looks unchanged - but the old Midland Bank has gone as has the TSB (just above the boat's stern) whilst the West of England Building Society has both gone and its building has been re-fronted. The way Bideford 'climbs' up the hill is shown well in this shot.

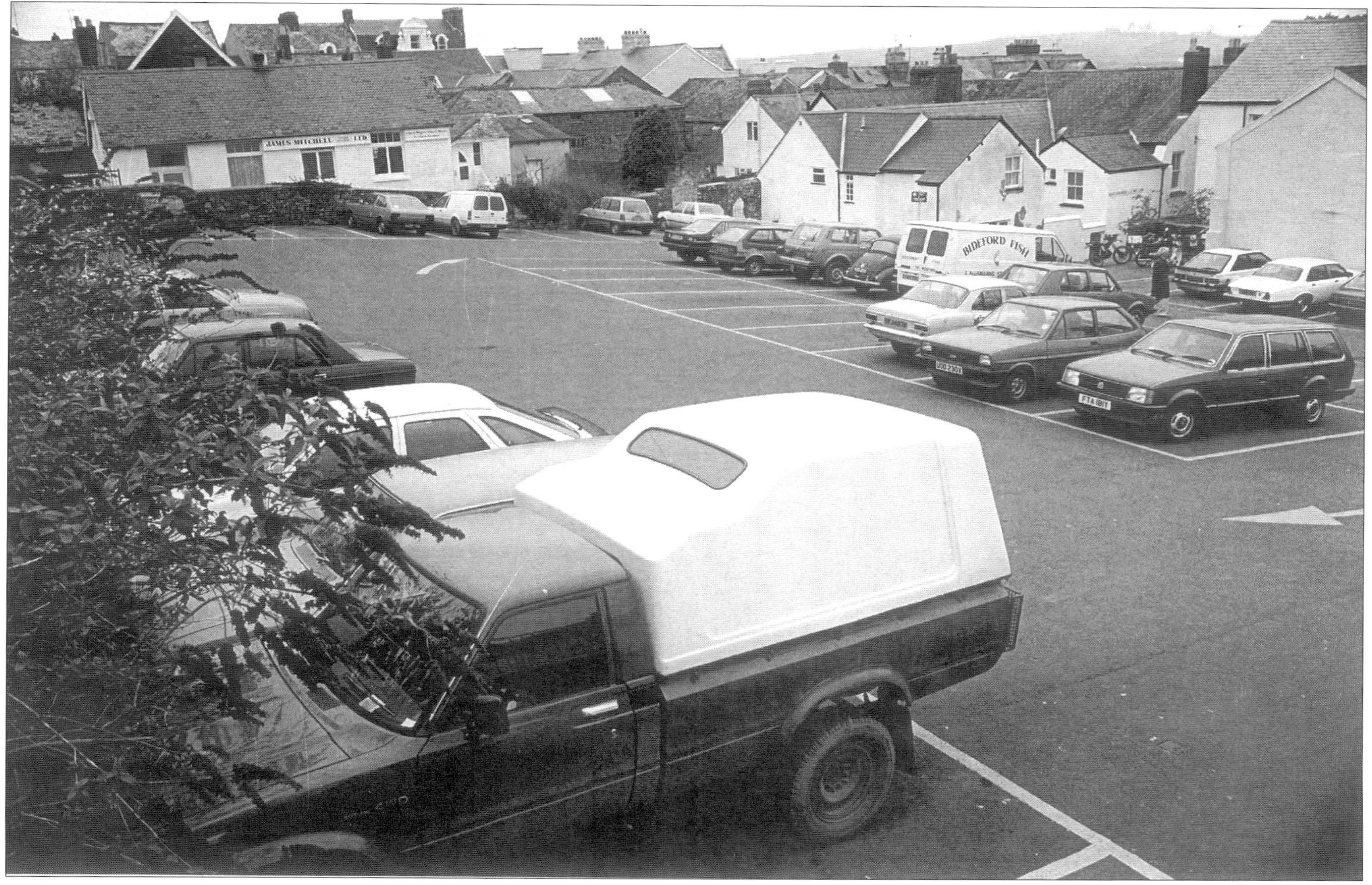

Apart from fashion nothing dates more quickly that cars - and here is a photograph from February 1986 to prove it. The shot is interesting as it also shows the old Wesleyan Sunday school building in use by James Mitchell Ltd., who made organs - and many of the buildings shown here have since been refurbished.

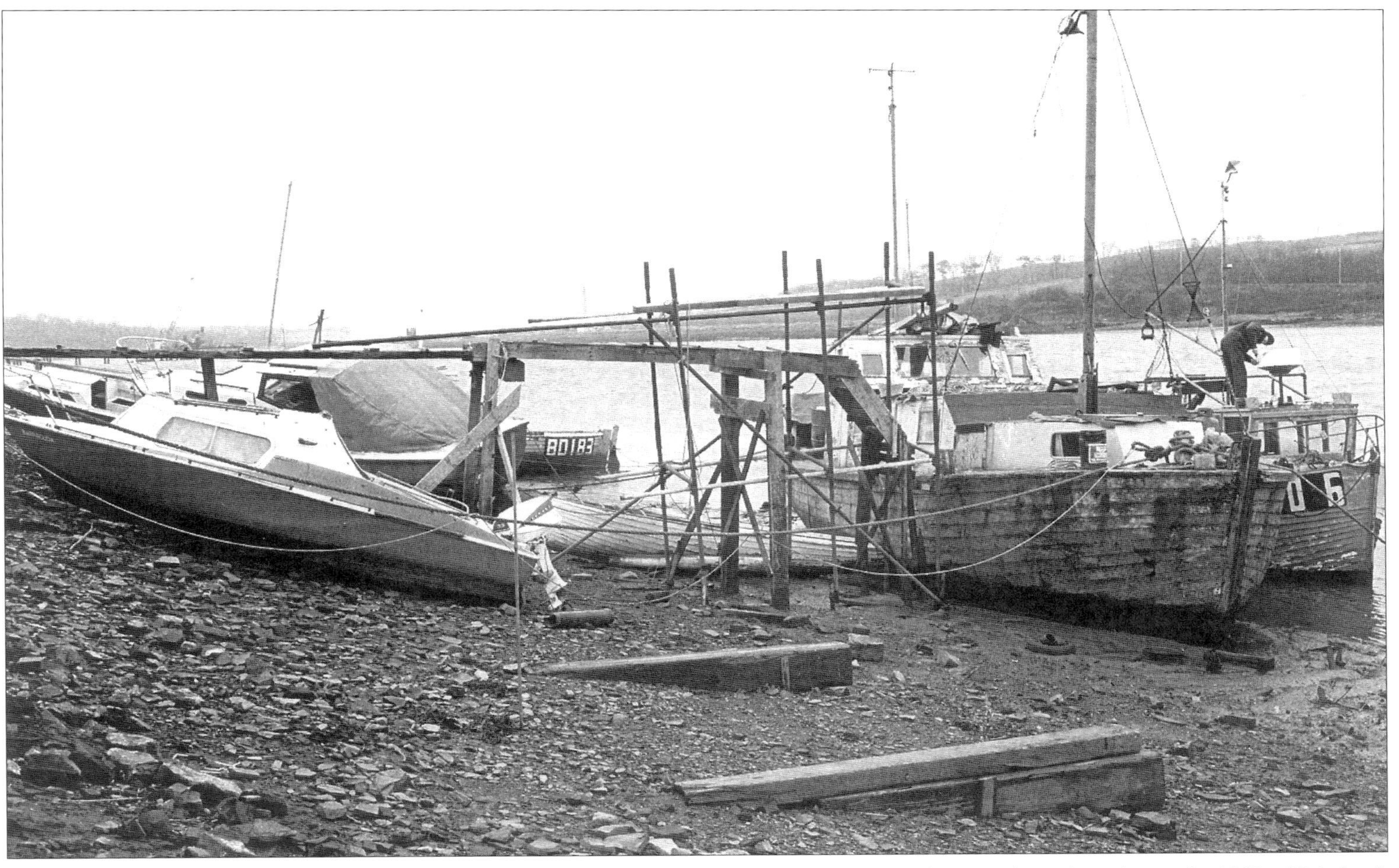

This rather ramshackle walkway was one of the ad-hoc developments that appeared at Bank End in the early 1980s. Bideford has long been a port but moorings for small boats are scarce and so owners migrated to this area - until Torridge district council put in hand a plan to sheet pile the river bank and begin charging for berths. The boat owners then all moved - to East-the-Water. The photograph dates from February 1986.

Council

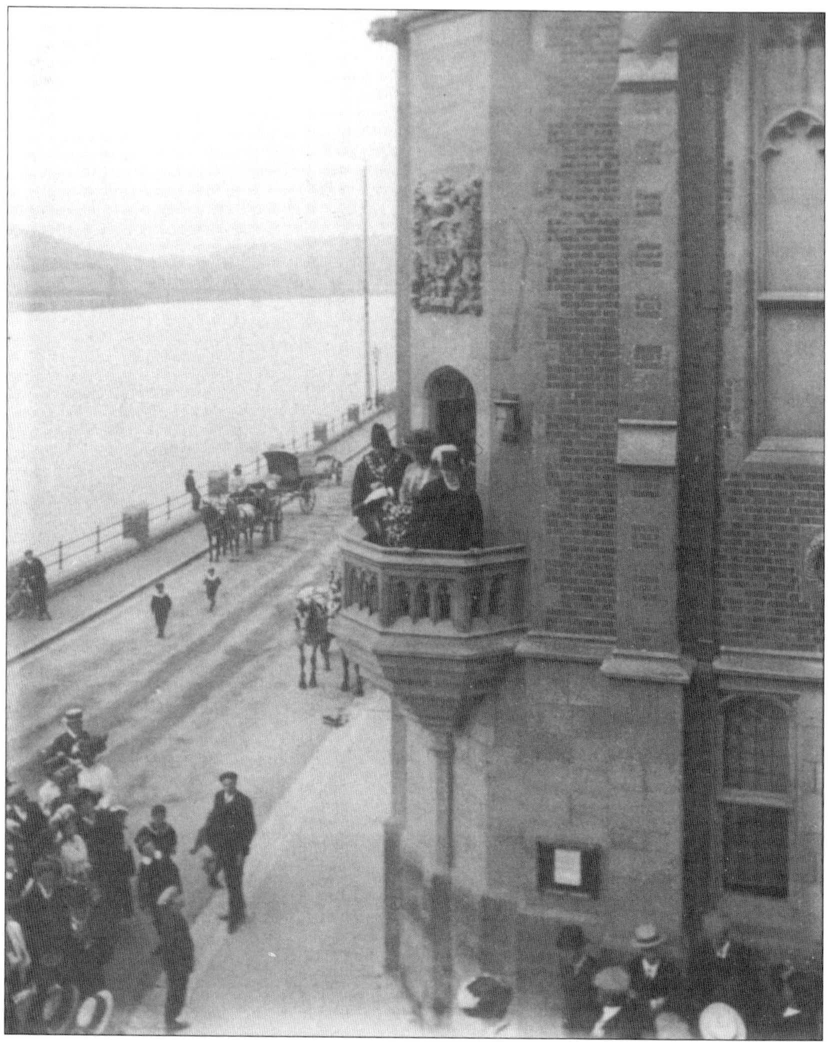

This view, taken from the Bridge Buildings, shows the small balcony on the corner of the Town Hall with the then Mayor plus a rather cramped group of dignitaries sometime before the First World War. What the occasion was and who the Mayor was I cannot say but note the absence of cars and the fact that the crowd are casually standing in the road - not something to be attempted lightly today.

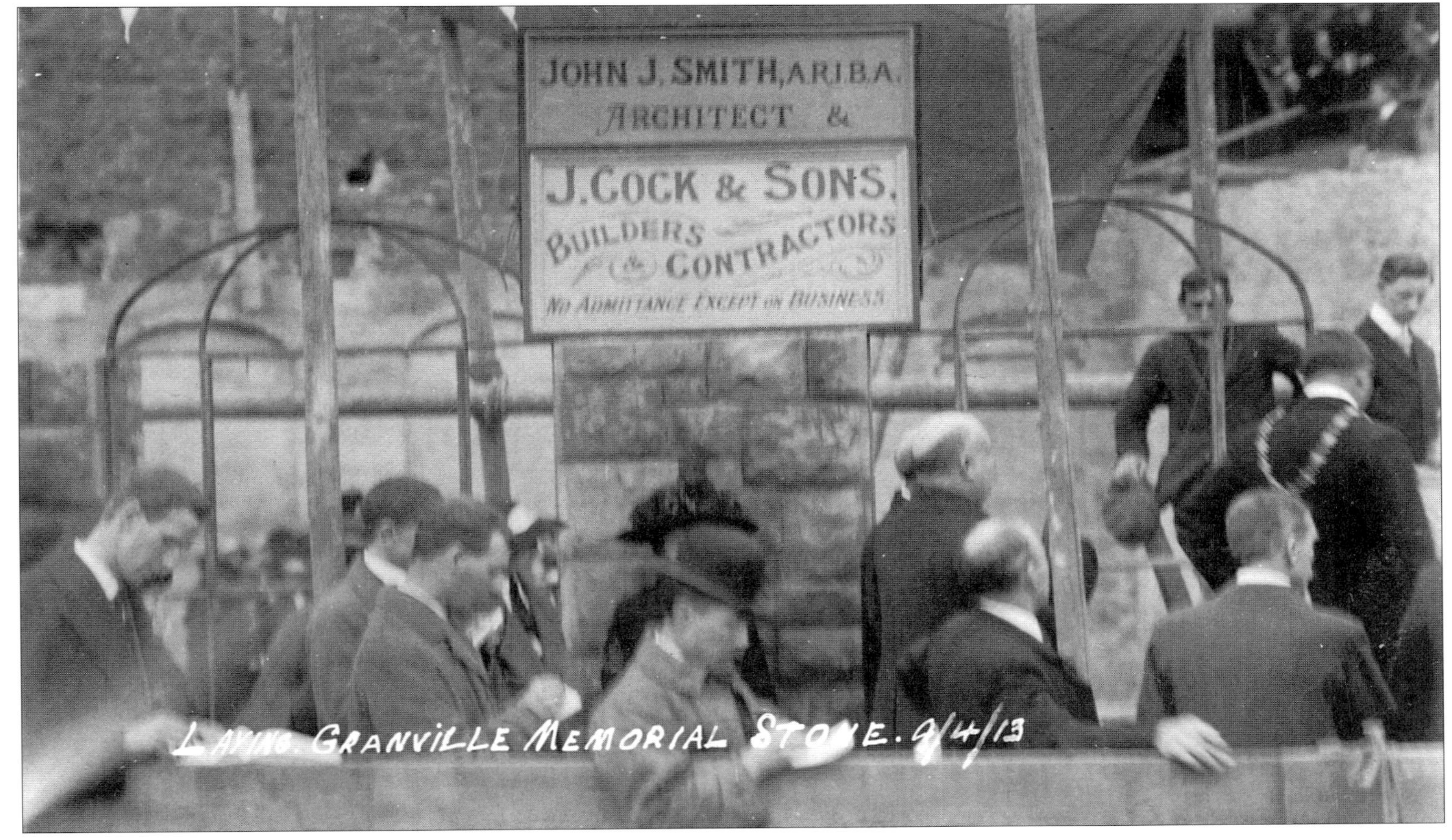

In Volume 1 of this series I printed a photograph of the stone-laying ceremony that marked the start of building of the Church Institute in Lower Meddon Street in April 1913. Since then I have been lent another picture showing the same scene but from a very different angle. The postcard is entitled 'Laying Granville memorial Stone 9/4/13' as the Institute was actually erected as a memorial to both the Grenville family and the late Victorian rector of Bideford the Reverend Roger Granville.

In *Illustrations of Old Bideford* Volume 1 I used two photographs taken in 1925 showing some of the events held to mark the opening of the new hospital in Abbotsham Road. The one now reproduced shows the committee plus doctors (or teachers) in their degree robes and mortar boards and the nursing staff - with the Mayor Dr.Toye in his chains of office to the right.

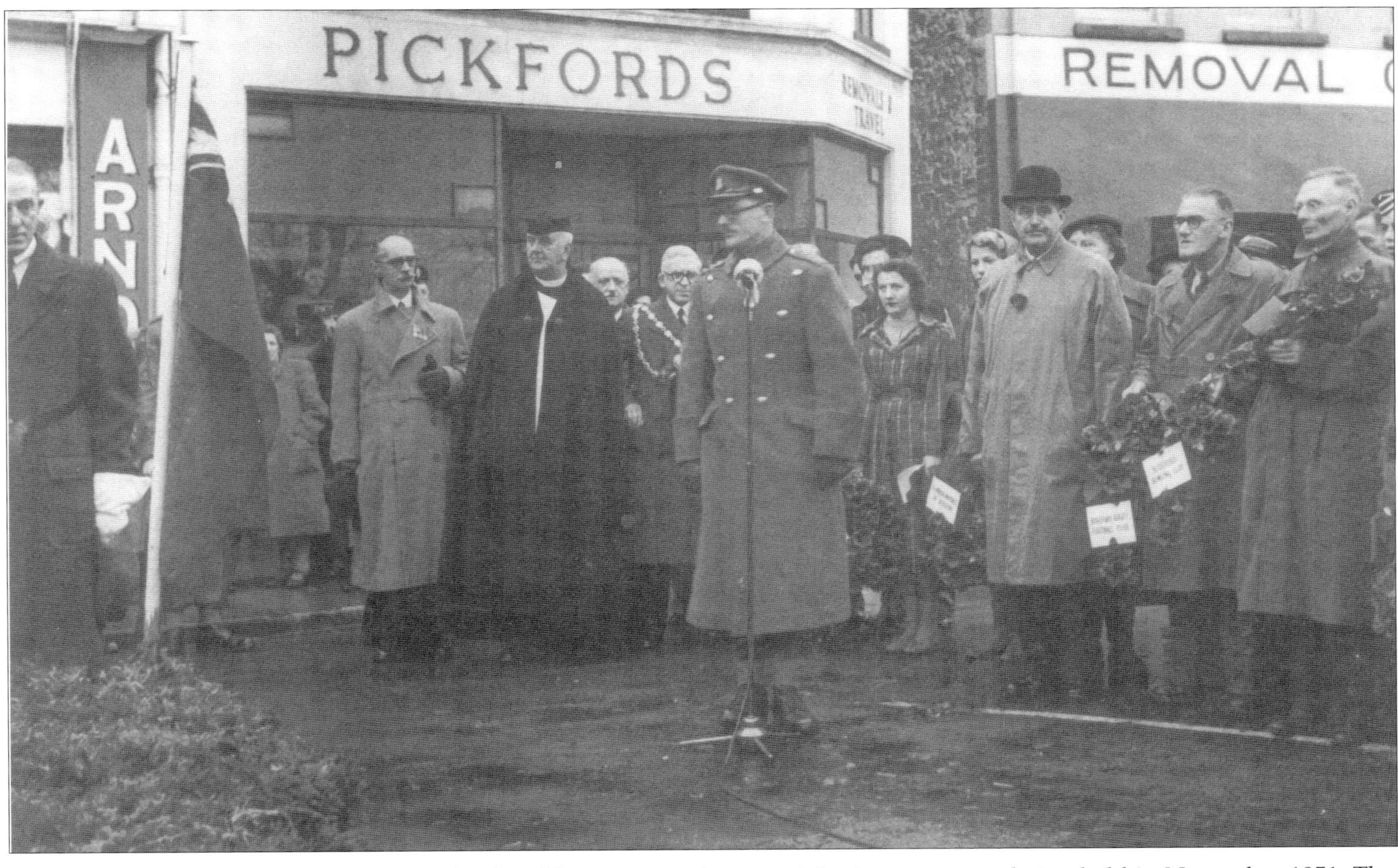

Bideford has always honoured its war dead and here we see the wreath laying ceremony being held in November 1951. The Mayor is WH Copp and the site is in front of what is today's Spice Restaurant and a bookmaker's shop

FESTIVAL OF BRITAIN
1951

Since seeing the 1951 Exhibition in London I am more than ever convinced of the worth-while nature of this really great effort. No doubt there are large numbers of people who do not agree that the present time is a suitable one, the main objection being the fact of our present financial difficulties, both personal and national, yet in spite of these facts it is still necessary for us to show the whole world, that far from being in a decadent condition, we are in a position to produce manufactured articles second to none—yes: and we *do* produce them!

Further: I think it well worth doing even under present conditions of life and living, because of its effect upon the morale of the people as a whole. Were we *all* to refuse to support this national effort it would shout to an astonished world:—" England has had to say ' Halt! we've had enough!! At last our enemies have triumphed and our heads are in the dust.' "

Let the Festival spirit continue. The time is not yet for England to bend the knee to circumstance!!!

Yours truly,

W. H. SHORT,
Mayor, 1950-51.

Bideford Motto:
" Pro Rege Ac Fide Audax "—Bold for King and Faith.

Following the Second World War Britain was a drab place with widespread bomb damage, on-going rationing and a lack of much to celebrate. To dispel this air of despondency it was decided to hold a 'Festival of Britain' in 1951. Communities across the country entered into this with great enthusiasm and Bideford wasn't left out. It staged various events through the year including concerts, plays, fetes, art exhibitions, a gymkhana and even a Trades Exhibition. A programme was printed and this illustration shows the foreword by the then Mayor W.H.Short.

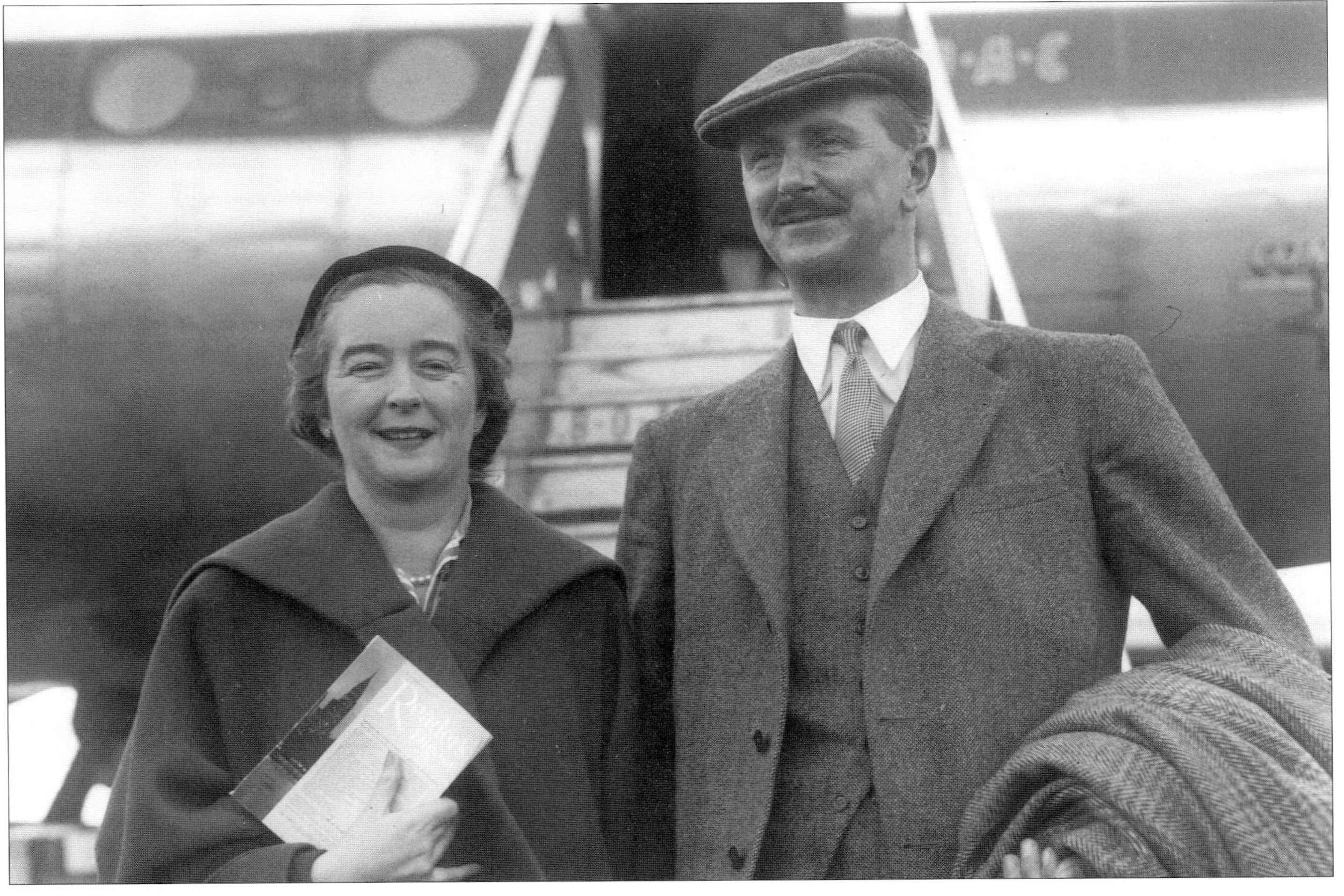

Over the years 1954-6 Sir Dennis Stucley of Hartland Abbey was elected Mayor of Bideford - even though he wasn't actually a councillor. During his time in office he undertook a visit to Biddeford in Maine, USA to take fraternal greetings to Bideford's daughter town. He is seen here with Lady Stucley just about to board a BOAC transatlantic passenger plane on his way to Bideford's namesake

Previous page: The annual election of the Mayor used to always be marked by a large parade on 'Mayor's Sunday' - and here we see a contingent of young men from the town's Sea Cadet Corps lined up outside Bridge Buildings in May 1956. Standing with their back to us is the Bideford Band. The Mayor in whose honour the parade was held was J.H.Sharley.

Above: Another shot of the Mayor's Parade in May 1956 shows a close-up of a band marching up to St.Mary's through the churchyard. Notice the 'Kingdom Hall' of the Jehovah's Witnesses to the left.

Next page: This photograph of some Bideford Girl Guides was snapped outside the King's Arms on the Quay on another Mayor's Sunday some five years later in 1961.

F. D. GODFREY

By the late 1950s complaints about the noisome and overcrowded nature of the old cattle market in Honestone Street led to its re-location to a new custom-built facility behind Victoria Park. As with the earlier site the Mayor of the day opened this and here we see councillor R.Lake in the auctioneer's section on the first day of business in 1960.

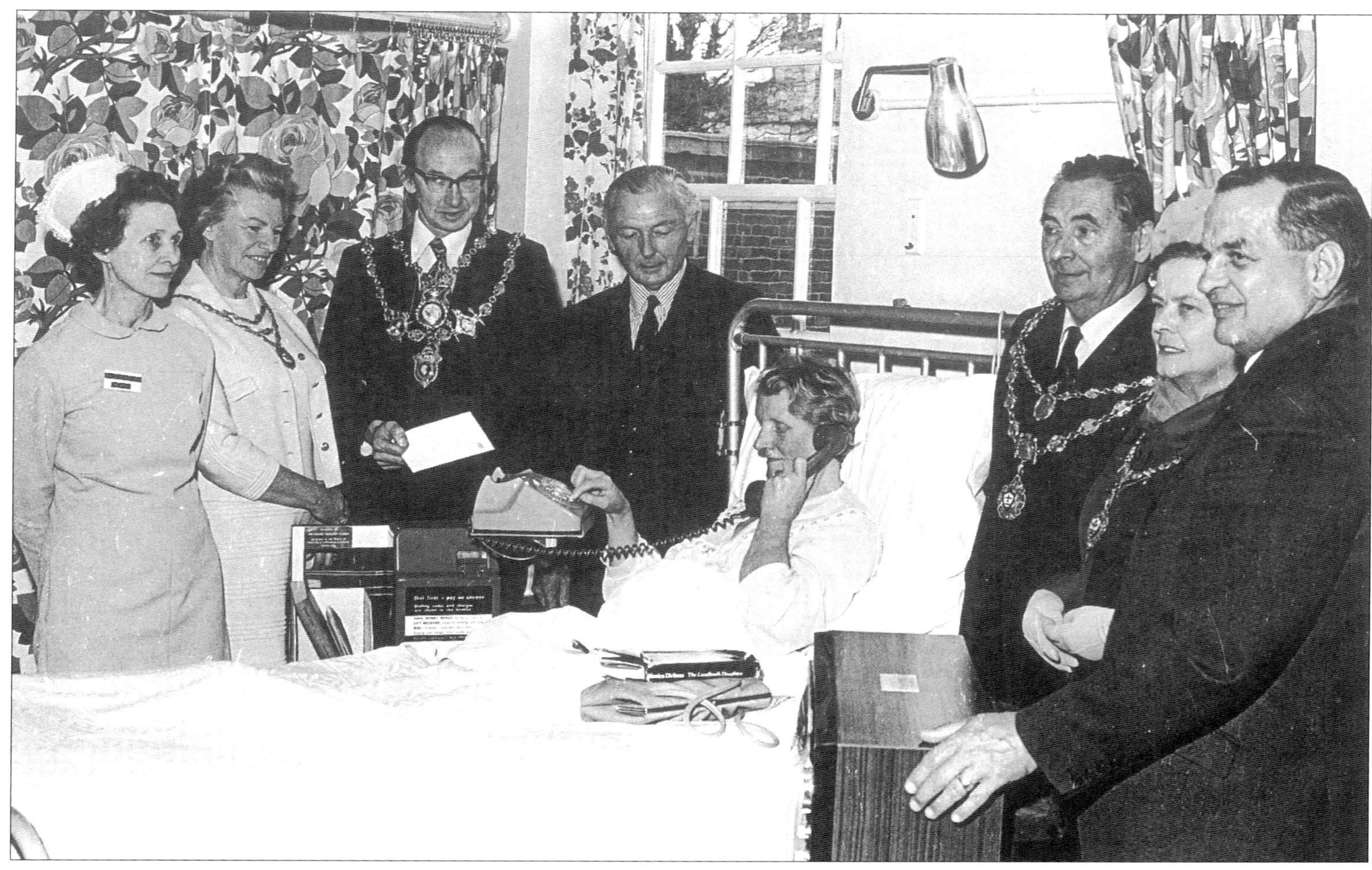

A rather formal telephone call is pictured here from May 1973. It was taken in Bideford Hospital and shows Mrs. M.Fripp of Braunton making the first call on the new 'bedside telephone service' which had been paid for by a public appeal mounted by the then Mayor Jim Needs who is standing to the left of the bed. The other Mayor, on the right, is Harold Pollard of Torrington who was there to present a new television set to the hospital.

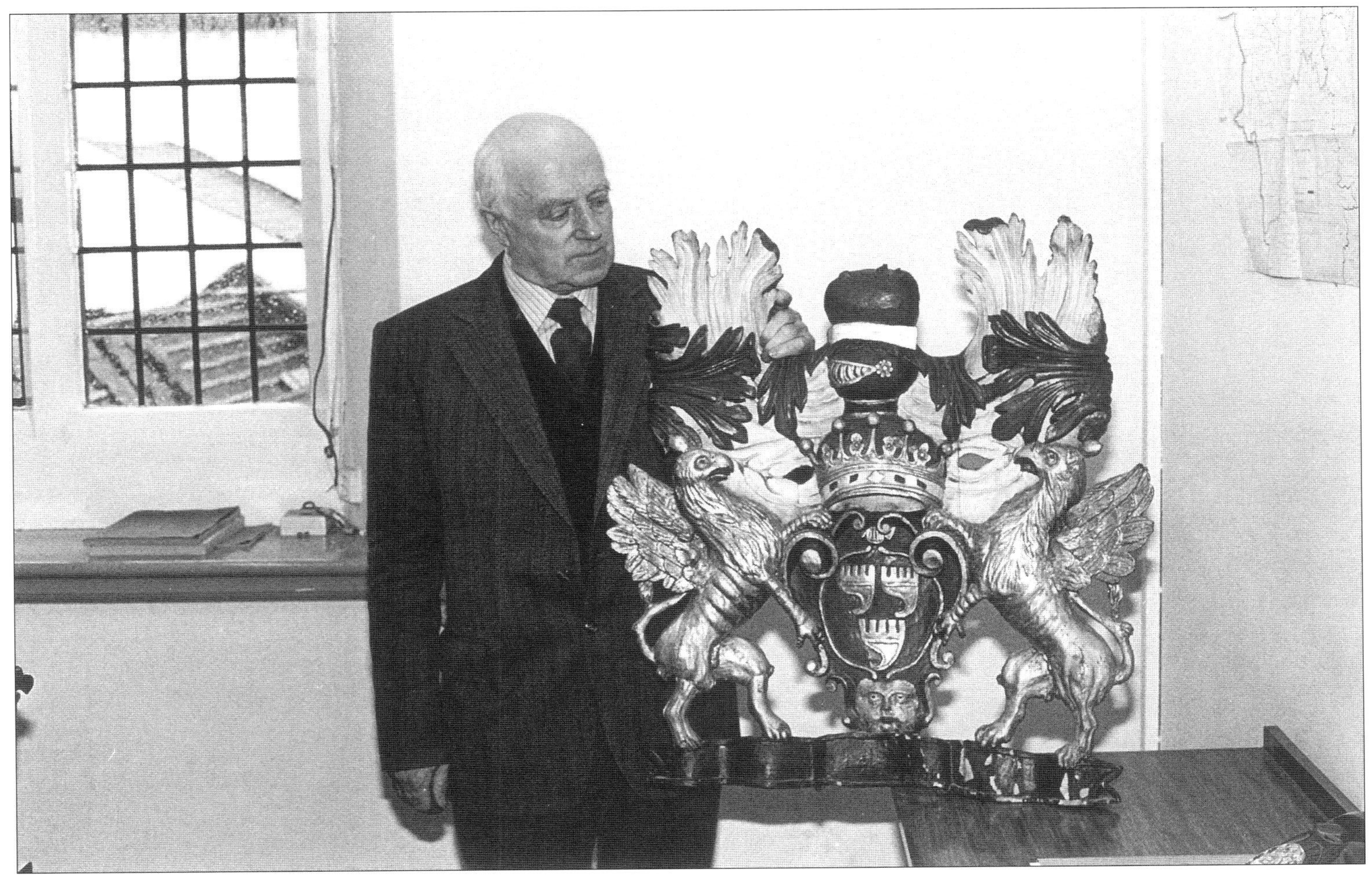

Ian Hay was town clerk of Bideford during much of the 1980s and he is seen here in January 1984 inspecting a newly refurbished and repainted Bideford coat-of-arms. The work was carried out by councillor Doug Vickers who, in his professional life, was a painter and decorator. The arms still hang proudly in the Town Hall.

Bideford town crier Jim Weeks is seen here in full voice announcing 'National No Smoking Day' in the Pannier Market in March 1987. The council had agreed to 'lend' him to help a health education programme in North Devon but the market traders in the picture do not seem to have got the message. They are from the left, Terry Trinder, Clifford Luggar, Barbara Trinder and Cynthia Luggar.

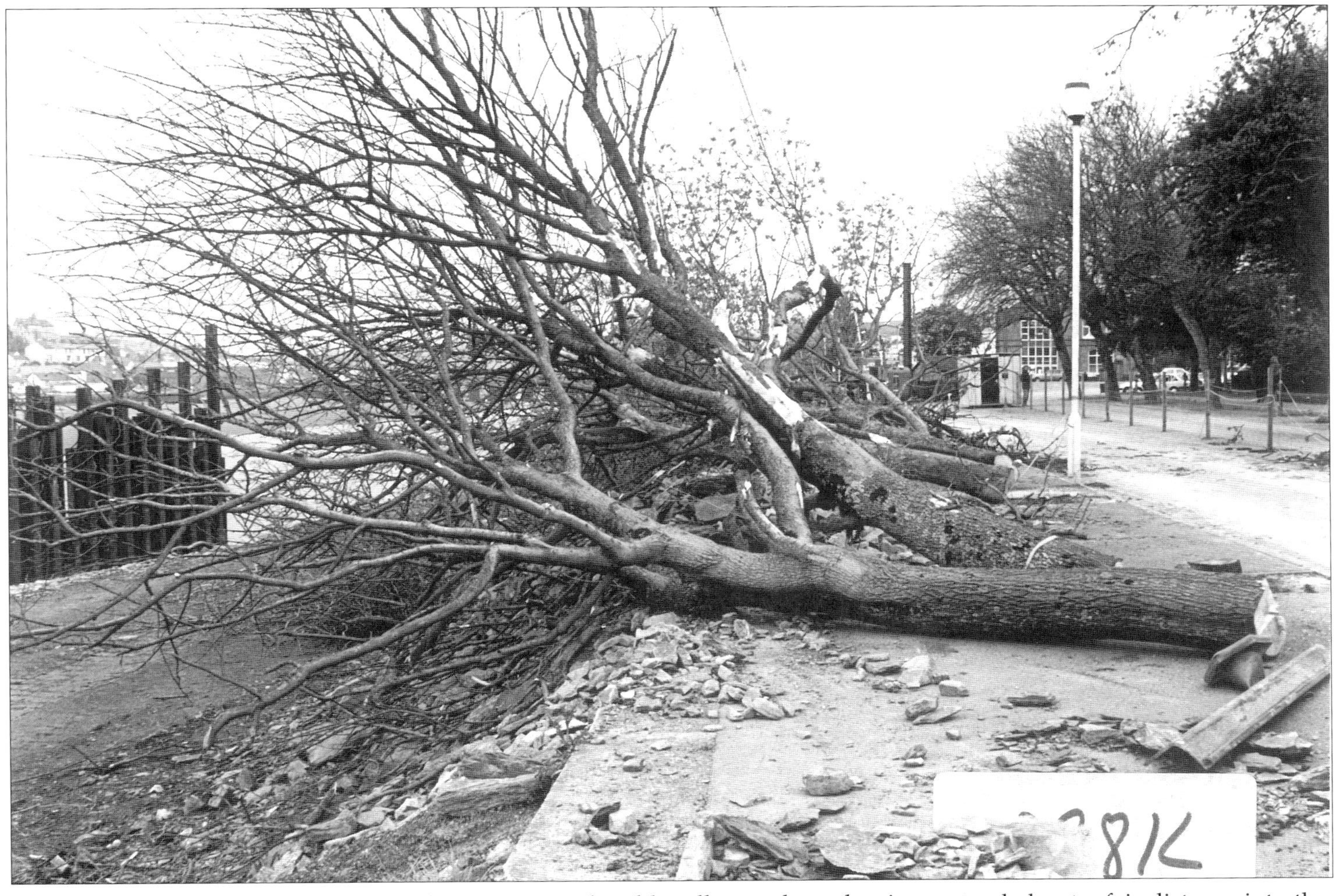

The building of the Riverbank car park in 1991 saw the old walkway along the river extended out a fair distance into the channel of the River Torridge. Unfortunately it also saw the cutting down of a much loved avenue of trees - as shown in this photograph. Their very unpopular removal co-incided with a council election which saw the Conservative chairman losing his seat to me partly on this issue.

Wartime

Above: Captain G.B.Oerton's rather large Army kit is seen here being loaded onto a South West Railway horse wagon before being taken to the Bideford railway station for passage to Bombay. Jubilee Square provides the backdrop - before the present day shop with its famous copper dome was erected. Captain Oerton went on to become a Lieutenant Colonel and he commanded the Barnstaple Home Guard in World War Two.

Next Page: This shot of an army parade along the Quay was probably taken just before the Second World War and I suspect these are members of the local Territorial force who were attached to the Devonshire regiment - and note that every man seems to be in step - and very smart they look too.

These doughty looking boys with their rakishly angled forage caps and rifles were pictured on the steps of Geneva School sometime just before the Second World War. They were the school's Cadet Force - many of whom entered the Home Guard when they were 16 before going on to join the regular forces a little later.

5th Batt. (Bideford) Home Guard.
No. 2 Platoon "B" Company, 1942.
Ptes. S. Laird, P. Cloke, W. E. Vodden, C. M. S. Gosling, Sgt. R. Featherstone, Pte. T. D. Frayne, Cpl. G. R. Hill
Ptes. F. J. Clements, G. Waldron, J. Lock, Cpl. F. Stacey, Pte. W. Raymont, Cpl. E. J. Moyes.
L/Cpls. F. D. Miles, F. Clarke, Cpl. R. C. Halbert, Cpl. R. Day, Ptes. C. Kelly, W. Weedon, J. Olver, Cpl. H. Mounce,
Ptes. S. J. Short, A. C. Waldon, E. Symonds, L. Braund, A. Tuplin, Cpl. A. Huxtable, Cpl. F. Rockey, Mr. E. Brown.
Sgt. S. Hawkins, Pte. R. Cade, Sgt. R. Northcote, Sgt. T. R. Harding, Major Cudmore, 2/Lt. W. H. Pascoe,
Lt. C. Brough, Capt. J. R. Ellis, 2/Lt. H. Sherbourne, Sgt. F. Clarke, Sgt. J. H. Hillman, Sgt. L. Short.
Ptes. R. Webb, C. Tryon, R. Raymont, L]Cpl. E. R. Youngs, Ptes. H. Lee, W. W. Horn, M. Vanstone, C. W. King,
Cpl. S. C. Smaldon.

Above: This photograph is self-explanatory and shows another group from the Bideford Home Guard to add to those I published in my previous two volumes. The very young boys present were receiving initial training in the Home Guard before moving on to join the regular forces.

Overleaf: The 2nd World War saw every community preparing for the worst. In Bideford the borough council had organised Air Raid Precautions from at least 2 years before hostilities actually broke out and in June 1941 they published a small booklet setting out 'What you should know. What you should do.' Reproduced here are four pages from it showing where the air raid shelters were located and the names and areas covered by some of the Air Raid Wardens.

6

Sector 2.—Northam Road, North View Avenue, Stanhope Terrace, Elmsdale Road, Sunningdale Terrace, Alexandra Terrace, Glendale Terrace, Newton Road.

Sector 3.—The Pill, Park Avenue, Park Lane, Elliott's Garage, Kingsley Road, Garden Theatre, B.A.R.C., New Site for P.O., New Cinema, Sports Ground, Chaplin's Garage.

WARDEN'S POST.—Messrs. J. Cock & Sons' Office, Kingsley Road (Tel. 87). Official Number of Post, ABi 12.

GROUP B.

Group Warden : E. B. Wrey, 18, Elm Grove.

Sector 4.—Beechcroft, Hazelhurst, Eyford, Pen Point, Cooleen, West Bank, Belvoir Road, Belvoir Terrace, Wimbourne Terrace, Lime Grove, Westcombe.

Sector 9.—Abbotsham Road, Ashley Terrace, Royston Road, Rectory, Dymond Road, Moreton Cottages.

WARDENS' POST.—Mr. Norman Chope's Garage at Brackenbrae, Belvoir Road (Tel. 91). Official Number of Post, ABi 13.

GROUP C.

Group Warden : A. C. Hancock, 34, Myrtle Grove.

Sector 5.—Chingswell Street, Willett Street, The Strand, Rope Walk, Mignonette Walk, Northdown Hall, R.C. Church, Woodland Terrace, Kingsley Street, North Road.

Sector 6.—Pitt Lane, " Iffield," Elm Grove, Hillside Terrace, Hillcroft Terrace, Myrtle Grove, Rockmount Terrace, 13 to 18, New Row ; Elmscott Terrace, Myrtle Gardens.

7

Sector 7.—Higher Gunstone, River View, 1 to 7, New Row ; Coldharbour, Florence Terrace, Lamerton Place, Lower Gunstone.

WARDENS' POST.—Gunstone School. Official Number of Post ABi 15.

GROUP D.

Group Warden : A. J. Lee, 3, Welbrook Terrace.

Sector 8.—Allhalland Street, Union Street, Mill Street, Cooper Street, Hart Street, Bridgeland Street, Quay (north from Bridge Chambers), King Street, Queen Street, Chapel Street.

WARDENS' POST.—Harbour Master's Office, The Quay (Tel. 321). Official Number of Post, ABi 14.

Sector 10.—High Street, Queen Annes, Pimlico, Providence Row, New Street.

Sector 16.—South from Town Hall, Tanton's Hotel, Hampton Terrace, Police Station, Lower Meddon Street, Bull Hill, Kingsley Terrace, Wellbrook Terrace, New Road, Torridge Hill, Northam Ridge, Church Walk, Bilton Terrace, Marine Gardens, Garfield Terrace.

WARDENS' POST.—British Legion Headquarters, New Street (Off High Street). Official Number of Post, ABi 16.

GROUP E.

Group Warden : J. W. Baker, 30a, Silver Street.

Sector 11.—Grenville Street, Market Place, Buttgarden Street, Bridge Street, Tower Hill, Victoria Terrace, Silver Street, Frederick Place.

WARDENS' POST.—Pannier Market. Official Number of Post, ABi 19.

Sector 13.—Honestone Street, Highfield, Victoria Gardens, Victoria Grove, Cattle Market.

6

Sector 2.—Northam Road, North View Avenue, Stanhope Terrace, Elmsdale Road, Sunningdale Terrace, Alexandra Terrace, Glendale Terrace, Newton Road.

Sector 3.—The Pill, Park Avenue, Park Lane, Elliott's Garage, Kingsley Road, Garden Theatre, B.A.R.C., New Site for P.O., New Cinema, Sports Ground, Chaplin's Garage.

WARDEN'S POST.—Messrs. J. Cock & Sons' Office, Kingsley Road (Tel. 87). Official Number of Post, ABi 12.

GROUP B.

Group Warden : E. B. Wrey, 18, Elm Grove.

Sector 4.—Beechcroft, Hazelhurst, Eyford, Pen Point, Cooleen, West Bank, Belvoir Road, Belvoir Terrace, Wimbourne Terrace, Lime Grove, Westcombe.

Sector 9.—Abbotsham Road, Ashley Terrace, Royston Road, Rectory, Dymond Road, Moreton Cottages.

WARDENS' POST.—Mr. Norman Chope's Garage at Brackenbrae, Belvoir Road (Tel. 91). Official Number of Post, ABi 13.

GROUP C.

Group Warden : A. C. Hancock, 34, Myrtle Grove.

Sector 5.—Chingswell Street, Willett Street, The Strand, Rope Walk, Mignonette Walk, Northdown Hall, R.C. Church, Woodland Terrace, Kingsley Street, North Road.

Sector 6.—Pitt Lane, " Iffield," Elm Grove, Hillside Terrace, Hillcroft Terrace, Myrtle Grove, Rockmount Terrace, 13 to 18, New Row ; Elmscott Terrace, Myrtle Gardens.

7

Sector 7.—Higher Gunstone, River View, 1 to 7, New Row ; Coldharbour, Florence Terrace, Lamerton Place, Lower Gunstone.

WARDENS' POST.—Gunstone School. Official Number of Post ABi 15.

GROUP D.

Group Warden : A. J. Lee, 3, Welbrook Terrace.

Sector 8.—Allhalland Street, Union Street, Mill Street, Cooper Street, Hart Street, Bridgeland Street, Quay (north from Bridge Chambers), King Street, Queen Street, Chapel Street.

WARDENS' POST.—Harbour Master's Office, The Quay (Tel. 321). Official Number of Post, ABi 14.

Sector 10.—High Street, Queen Annes, Pimlico, Providence Row, New Street.

Sector 16.—South from Town Hall, Tanton's Hotel, Hampton Terrace, Police Station, Lower Meddon Street, Bull Hill, Kingsley Terrace, Wellbrook Terrace, New Road, Torridge Hill, Northam Ridge, Church Walk, Bilton Terrace, Marine Gardens, Garfield Terrace.

WARDENS' POST.—British Legion Headquarters, New Street (Off High Street). Official Number of Post, ABi 16.

GROUP E.

Group Warden : J. W. Baker, 30a, Silver Street.

Sector 11.—Grenville Street, Market Place, Buttgarden Street, Bridge Street, Tower Hill, Victoria Terrace, Silver Street, Frederick Place.

WARDENS' POST.—Pannier Market. Official Number of Post, ABi 19.

Sector 13.—Honestone Street, Highfield, Victoria Gardens, Victoria Grove, Cattle Market.

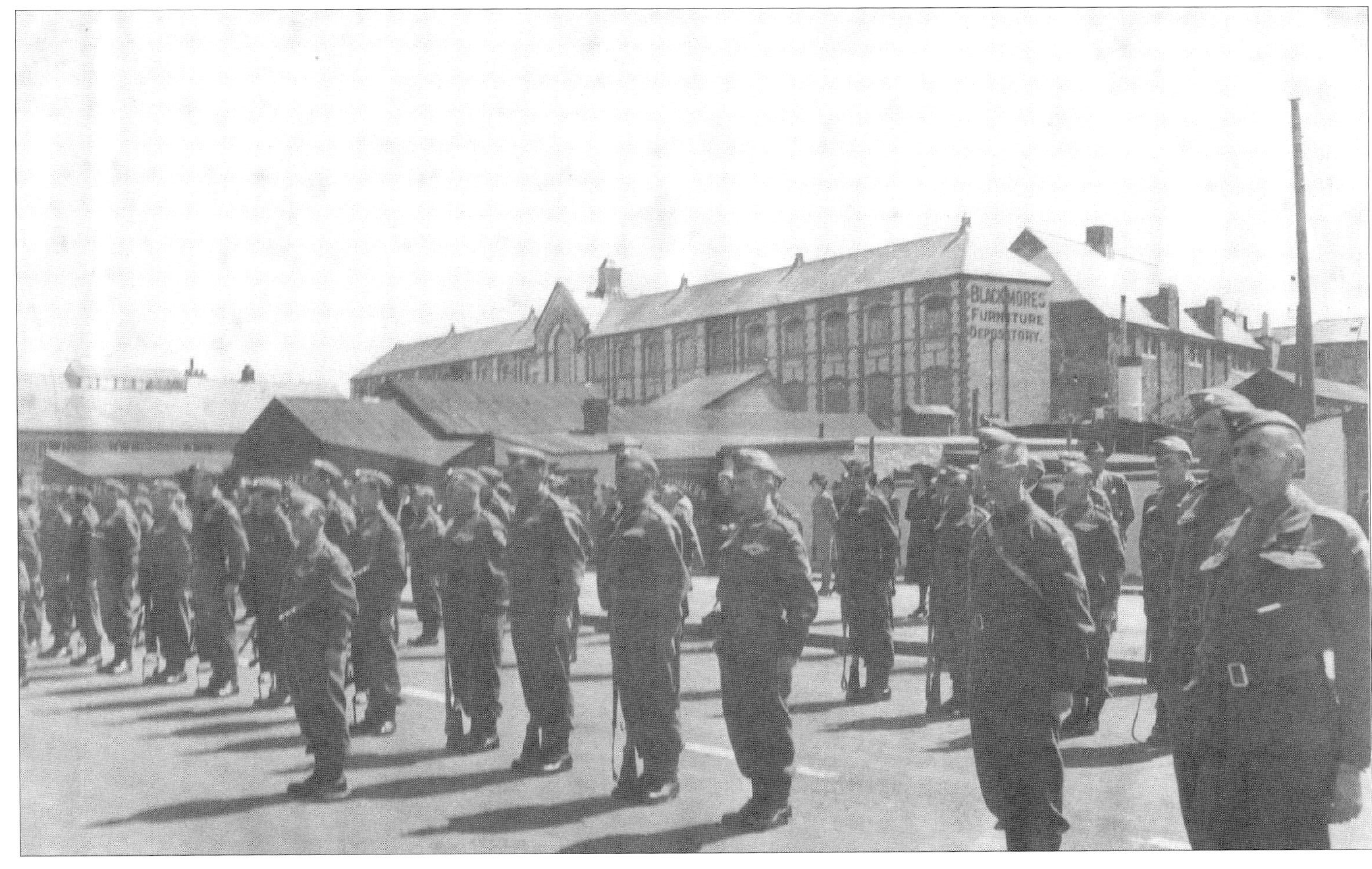

This photograph could be clearer but it is a rare shot showing many of the 750 strong 5th (Bideford) Battalion of the Home Guard on parade on the Pill in 1944.

In the first volume of this series I printed a photograph of D Company of the Bideford Home Guard marching along the Quay. This shot shows B Company in the same parade in October 1944 and I have to say they do not look like the 'amateurs' portrayed in 'Dad's Army'.

This and the following two fine photographs of the Bideford Home Guard come from the personal collection of William Pascoe who was a 2nd Lieutenant in the force. *Above*: shows some of the men outside Leonard's coal stores which was below the extension to Tanton's Hotel on New Road.

The second (*next page*) was taken this time outside Tanton's I think and shows some fascinating details of the unit's uniform and armaments - especially the sub-machine gun being casually held by the man on the right. I assume the V-sign being made by the man on the left was a 'V for Victory' rather than its more basic meaning - though he is doing it the 'wrong' way round if he is copying Churchill's famous gesture.

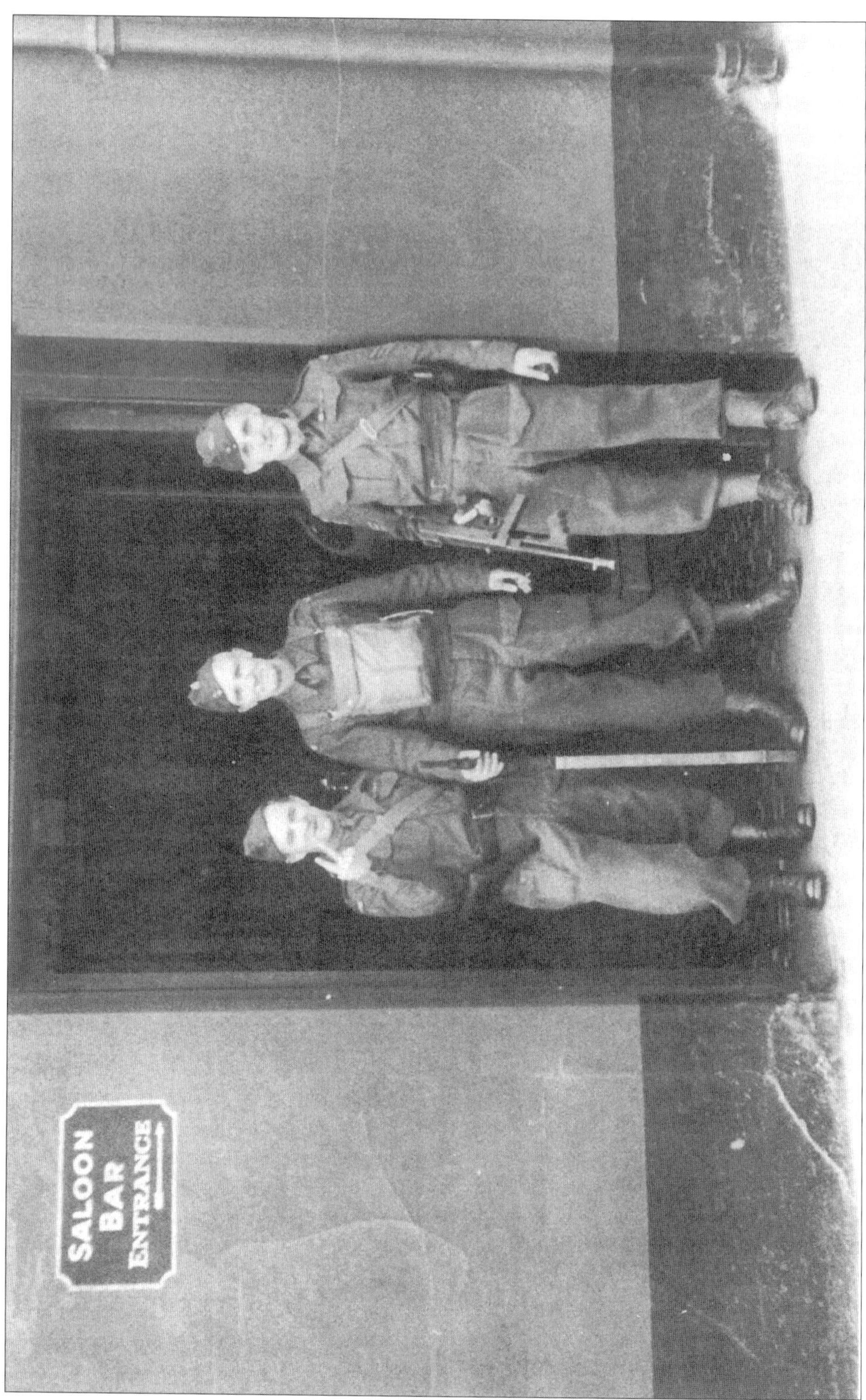
SALOON
BAR
ENTRANCE

The third shot from the personal collection of William Pascoe shows four men of the Bideford Home Guard running a field kitchen at Cornborough in Abbotsham. If an army marches on its stomach then the Bideford unit seem to have been well catered for.

Another shot of the Bideford Home Guard pictured on the Quay in front of the now demolished toilets. Some attempt seems to have been made to obscure the words 'Port of Bideford' - presumably to confuse the Nazis if they had invaded the town! The large ship to the right was one of the many freighters delivering supplies to the US and British troops training in the area.

Salvage! For Victory!!

WASTE PAPER, METALS, TINS, and BONES ARE URGENTLY REQUIRED

The waste paper collection will continue as at present. Collection of bones is being arranged. Particulars later.

ALUMINIUM ARTICLES should be taken or sent to the W.V.S. Depot at the Manor Yard. Entrance on Pill Road.

For a week commencing Thursday, 18th July, metal and tins will be collected by authorised lorry following a programme as set out below, or any scrap metal can be left at the Salvage Depot, Manor Yard (entrance Quay Road). Large quantities will be collected by arrangement or on receipt of post-card by the Borough Surveyor. Profits will be given to the Government

Thursday and Friday 18th and 19th July	Area: High Street and southwards to Landcross Bridge (including Old Town and Clovelly Road District).
Monday and Tuesday 22nd and 23rd July	Northwards from High Street to Cleavehouses (including Abbotsham Road, Belvoir, and Chanters Road District).
Wednesday and Thursday 24th and 25th July	East-the-Water

By Order of the Town Council,

F. C. BACKWAY, *Town Clerk*.

16th July, 1940

GAZETTE PRINTING SERVICE

This leaflet was printed by the old *Bideford Gazette* in 1940 during the darkest days of the Second World War when Britain was fearing invasion at any moment. Civilians were being urged to collect material useful to the war effort - a drive that eventually led to the disappearance of many ornamental railings which, sadly, have never been replaced.

Sport & Entertainment

Above: This photograph probably dates from before World War One and shows the original green of the Bideford Bowling Club before it moved across the road. The site later provided the land for the Garden Theatre on the Pill whilst the long white wall behind the bowlers has been replaced by a terrace of houses along the Strand.

Opposite page: Unfortunately this shot has no information with it other than it was taken in Bideford and shows one of the town's rowing clubs. It probably dates from around 1895-1900 and shows that though clothes and hair styles may have changed greatly the basic shape of the boats is still much the same today as it was then.

Bideford Regatta can be traced back into the middle of the nineteenth-century and as time went on so they became larger and steadily more supported. This panoramic shot from around 1900 shows the river crowded with rowers and their boats - with some well laden vessels packed with onlookers. Note the railway goods yard acting as a backdrop to this busy river scene. The basic shape of the boats is still much the same today as it was then.

BIDEFORD REGATTA.

AUGUST 16, 1883.

PROGRAMME OF RACES,

PRICE 3d.

1st Race. Four-oared Boats, employed in Salmon Fishery, with Nets.

1st PRIZE, £3; 2nd, £2; 3rd, £1.

"SUCCESS" (Appledore; *White*).—R. Courtice, T. Powe, J. Bowden, G. Cole (stroke).
"PHILLIP" (Appledore; *Red*).—J. Jenkins, R. Bowden, F. Gorrall, W. Jenkins (stroke).
"JAMES" (Appledore; *Blue*).—John Berry, J. Berry, W. Berry, W. Cox (stroke).

2nd Race. Four-oared Gigs, rowed by Amateurs, Silver Cups, value 15 Guineas.

1st PRIZE, Silver Goblet value Ten Guineas; 2nd, Silver Goblet value Five Guineas.

EXETER A. R. CLUB (*Blue*).—A. Rowe, F. Pike, C. C. Horsley, F. J. Sewell (stroke), B. Bowden (cox).
BIDEFORD ROWING CLUB (*Crimson and Black*).—W. Cox, T. Robins, W. Davey, W. Herniman (stroke), F. Shute (cox).
BARNSTAPLE ROWING CLUB (*Black and Amber*).—A. F. Seldon, W. A[illegible], T. R. Seldon, H. Westacott (stroke), W. Lewis (cox).
"EDITH" (Vulcan Rowing Club, Bideford; *Red and White*).—C. Waldron, H[illegible] Waldron, T. Backway, J. Davis (stroke), S. Down (cox).

3rd Race. Four-oared Gigs, Open, 1st prize, 12 guis.; 2nd, £6 6s.; 3rd, £3 3s.

BIDEFORD (*Crimson and black*).—W. Short, W. Isaacs, L. Shute, R. Herniman (stroke), F. Shute (cox).
DEVONPORT (*Black*).—Dawe, Tambling, Hockin, S. Sawdy (stroke), F. Balkwell (cox).
"BRISTOL" (Bristol; *Red*).—E. Hodgson, J. Hodgson, W. Bush, S. Bush (stroke), E. Hodgson (cox).
"EDITH" (Vulcan Rowing Club, Bideford; *Red and white*).—A. Symons, W. Gregory, H. Mountjoy, W. Davis (stroke), S. Down (cox).
"TAW VALE" (Barnstaple; *Black and Amber*).—S. Lewis, G. Gordon, J. Greenwood, J. Ratcliffe (stroke), A. Greenwood (cox).

This Regatta programme dates from 1883

4th Race. Pair-oared Gigs, rowed by Amateurs; Silver Cups, value 10 guineas.

1st PRIZE, Silver Goblet value Six Guineas; 2nd, Silver Medal value Three Guineas; 3rd, value One Guinea.

EXETER A. R. CLUB (*Blue*).—C. C. Horsley, F. P. Pike (stroke).
"NORA" (Vulcan Rowing Club, Bideford; *Red and White*).—T. Backway, J. Davis (stroke).
EXETER A. R. CLUB (*Red*).—F. J. Sewell, A. Rowe (stroke), B. Bowden (cox).
BARNSTAPLE ROWING CLUB (*Black and Amber*).—H. Westacott, A. F. Seldon (stroke), W. Lewis (cox).

5th Race. Pair-oared Gigs, Open; 1st Prize, £5; 2nd, £3; 3rd, £1.

"SILVIA" (Bristol; *Red*). J. Hodgson, W. Bush (stroke).
"NORA" (Vulcan Rowing Club, Bideford; *Red and White*).—H. Mountjoy, W. Davis (stroke).
BIDEFORD (*Dark Blue*).—S. Short, W. Parsons (stroke).
DEVONPORT (*Blue and White*).—T. Hocking, R. Tambling (stroke).
BIDEFORD (*Light Blue*).—R. Herniman, L. Shute (stroke), F. Shute (cox).
BIDEFORD (*Crimson and Black*).—W. Isaacs, W. Short (stroke).
"TAW VALE" (Barnstaple; *Black and amber*).—S. Lewis, J. Greenwood (stroke), A. Greenwood (cox).
"BRISTOL" (Bristol; *White*).—E. Hodgson, S. Bush (stroke).

GIG AND PUNT CHASE.—WINNER, 15s.; LOSER, 5s.
GIG, Arnold and Crew. PUNT, C. Lee Hutchings.

Neapolitan Pole Dance. Display of Fireworks, 9.30 p.m.

☞ *All Money Prizes will be paid at the conclusion of the Race. The other Prizes will be presented by G. W. VINCENT, Esq., the Mayor, at the Supper to be held in the Evening of the same day at Tanton's Hotel, at 7.30.*

Programme of Music to be played by the Band of the 4th D.R.V.

OVERTURE ... "In Memoriam" ... F. NEWTON.
FANTAZIA. "The Royal Musketeers" MULLOT.
ROMANZA...... "The Wanderer" ......H. ROUND.
SERENADE... "The Evening Star" ...H. ROUND.
VALSE... ..."Light and Shade"... .. H. ROUND.
GRAND SELECTION "Pirates of Penzance" ARTHUR SULLIVAN.
QUADRILLE "The Merry Changes" E. F. WILSON.
GLEE..... "The Forest Queen" ......H. ROUND.
OVERTURE ... "Knight Templar" ... H. ROUND.
VALSE .. .. "My Queen" ... ...COOTE.
EUPHONIUM SOLO... "Cavatina" ... ...BALFE.
QUADRILLE ... "Inspiration" ... ...SMITH.
RECIT. AND AIR | "The Death of Nelson"
TRUMBONE SOLO | [BRAHAM.
OVERTURE ..."Confidence"... ... J. HEMMELE.

GOD SAVE THE QUEEN.

BY ORDER OF THE COMMITTEE,
MR. C. FITTOCK (Lloyd's Surveyor), Starter.
MR. GEORGE POLLARD, Umpire.
THOS. LUSCOMBE, Hon. Sec.

[*Coles, Printer, Bideford*

It shows many names familiar in Bideford today

Above : An unusual viewpoint for this shot. Taken from the railway bridge at East-the-Water we see a hunt meeting sometime around 1920 with the Swan Inn as a backdrop. The shop to the left of the pub was demolished by Torridge district council some years ago and the space created used to extend the Royal Hotel car park. The ornate roof on the left was over the steps leading up to the station.

Opposite : Boxing has been going on in Bideford for many years and the local club has hopes to move into new premises at Pollyfield in the future so it should continue for many years yet. This programme shows a 1924 tournament held under the auspices of the Royal and Ancient Order of Buffaloes - a self-help Friendly Society which was still going in Bideford up until the 1970s in what is today Friendship House opposite the Pannier Market. Note the advertisement for the Palladium Cinema in Mill Street - Patt's greengrocery shop is the old entrance lobby.

NOTE.

C. WALDON

CABINET MAKER
UPHOLSTERER
AND POLISHER,

44, HONESTONE STREET,
BIDEFORD.

PICKARD'S DAIRY,

PROPRIETOR, G. TURNER.

NOTED FOR FINEST DEVONSHIRE CREAM,

SENT BY POST TO ALL PARTS

54, HIGH STREET,
BIDEFORD.

W. SLADE,

HOUSE DECORATOR,

PAINTS, OILS,
VARNISHES, &
PATTERN BOOKS

ALWAYS IN STOCK.

21, PITT LANE, BIDEFORD.

BRIGHT'S

FOR

STATIONERY,
BOOKS AND
FANCY GOODS,

ETC.

THE QUAY,
BIDEFORD.

PROGRAMME 2d EACH.

H. P. WOODYATT,

GROCER - -
AND - - - -
PROVISION
MERCHANT.

41, HIGH STREET, BIDEFORD.

R.A.O.B.

BOXING TOURNAMENT

AT BIDEFORD MARKET,

on

Whit-Monday, June 9, 1924.

Judges: COL. C. B. JAMES, GAY B. DENT. | REF.: H. P. WOODYATT, TIMEKEEPER: E. GRIMES.

DOORS OPEN 7 O'CLOCK. COMMENCING 7.45.

L. BRAUND,

FLORIST, FRUITERER
AND SEEDSMAN,

71, HIGH STREET, BIDEFORD.

A. TOTTLE

Hairdresser and
Tobacconist.

UMBRELLAS RECOVERED.

53, MILL STREET, BIDEFORD.

DAIRYMAN

T. CLEVERDON,

BIDEFORD.

CONTRACTOR.

THE

PALLADIUM

MILL STREET.

GOOD PICTURES AND MUSIC

7.30 NIGHTLY.

(2 Houses Saturdays and Holidays).

F. P. LEE,

ROPE WALK
COAL STORES,

BIDEFORD.

BEST HOUSE COAL,
COKE, WOOD, ETC,

AT ROCK BOTTOM PRICES.

PROGRAMME.

6 ROUND CONTEST:

C. PHILLIPS v J. WILLIAMS,
BIDEFORD. APPLEDORE.

6 ROUND RETURN CONTEST:

F. ANDREWS v W. HANAFORD
EXETER. (Previous Contest a Draw). EXETER.

GRAND 10 ROUND CONTEST:

TOM IND v BOY WILLS
BRISTOL. Winner of a Welter Weight Competition, National Sporting Club, out of 33 entries.
EXMOUTH. Winner of many contests and a Coming Champion. IN THE RING AT 8.45.

SPECIAL 10 ROUND CONTEST:

R. NEW v J. POWE
BARUM. Well known local 9st. Boxers. APPLEDORE.

6 ROUND RETURN CONTEST:

N. SNELLING v H. JINKS
PAIGNTON.—Fought a stubborn contest on May 14th at Exeter.—PLYMOUTH.

Other Contests time permitting.

MOTOR CARS
FOR HIRE.

OPEN OR CLOSED.

PHONE 94.

E. W. NICKSON

Automobile Engineer.

PRIVATE ADDRESS:

63 HIGH STREET,
BIDEFORD.

R. KEATES

HIGH CLASS
TOBACCONIST &
NEWS AGENT.

49, MILL STREET, BIDEFORD.

T.W.

T. WOODYATT,

GENTS'
TAILOR & OUTFITTER

FIT & WEAR GUARANTEED WITH EVERY SUIT.

42, TOP OF HIGH STREET,
BIDEFORD.

T.W.

A. LEWIS

High Class Ladies'
and Gents'

FOOTWEAR

Repairs given Special Attention.

Mill Street, Bideford.

This was the Bideford Park Rangers Football Club pictured around 1920. They were (back row, left to right), E.Brown, D.Ford, F.Tucker, J.Bale, R.J.Backway; (centre) J.Green, J.Little, T.Taylor, S.Farleigh; (front) W.Johns, A.Hambly, M.Woolf. Could the goal-keeper's flat cap be any bigger?

The Bideford Amateur Athletics Club had a variety of sections - rowing, athletics and football teams. The First XI from 1925-6 are seen here in their club room on the Pill. The inscription across the top of the photograph notes that they were runners-up in the North Devon Senior League in that year.

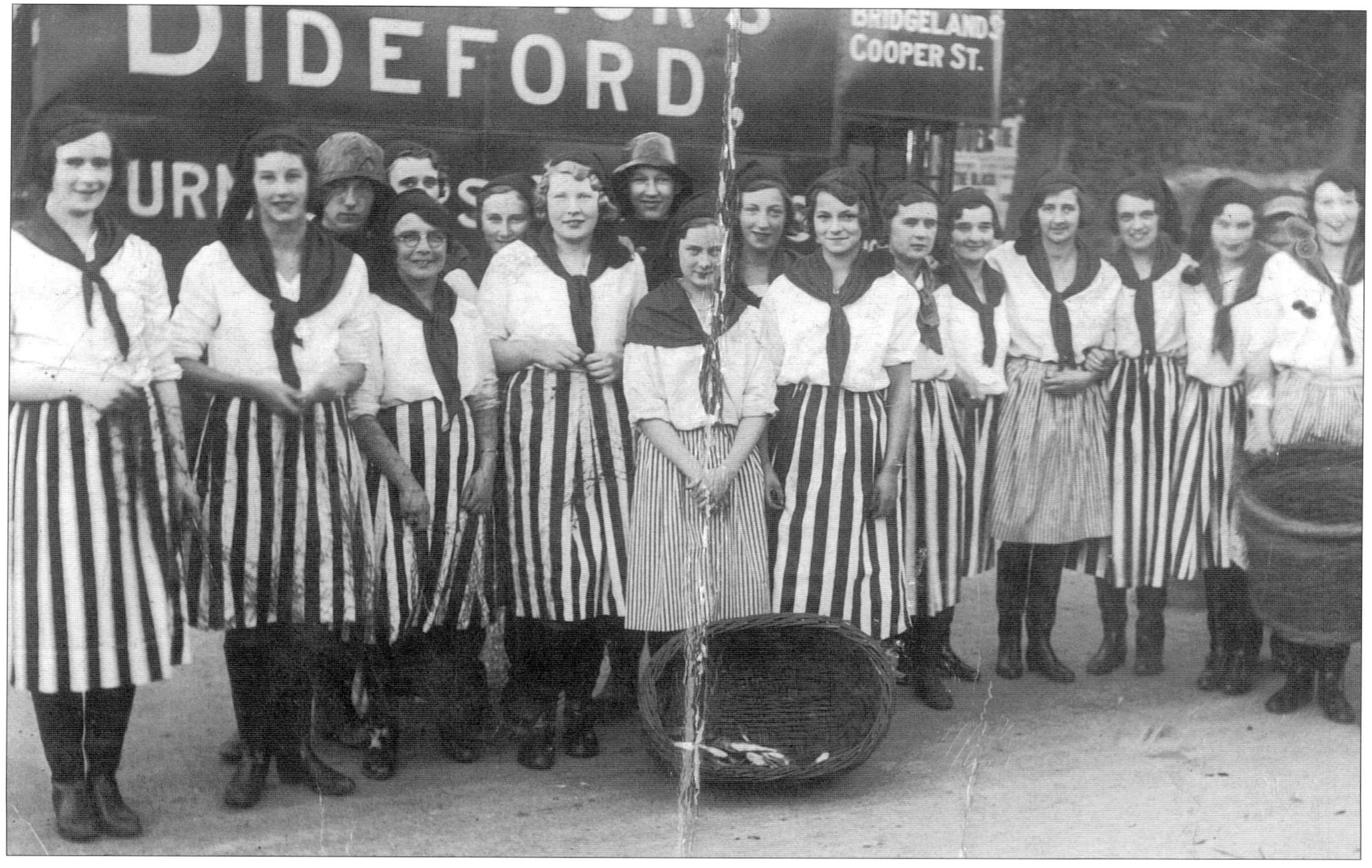

I do not know the date of this carnival photograph but I would estimate it to be from the 1930s. Pictured here are members of staff from Heywood's drapery shop dressed as herring girls (possibly meant to be from Clovelly?). Behind them stands the Braddick's furniture and removal van shown on page 87.

Before television and radio came to dominate our entertainment life Britain's towns could all boast many dance bands who played at the numerous local dances. Here we see the Golden Bay Dance Orchestra who were based in Bideford in the 1920s and 1930s. Note the bow ties and dinner jackets - I don't know what their music sounded like but they certainly looked smart

In 1951 the annual Bideford Regatta was held before huge crowds even though the day was marked by drizzling rain. An innovation on that day was the use of ex-Army walkie-talkie radio sets by marshals to help control the events. The four young men who volunteered to use them are shown here standing on a rather wet Quay. The one on the right is thought to be Roger Day who went on to run Sudbury's Gloves in the town.

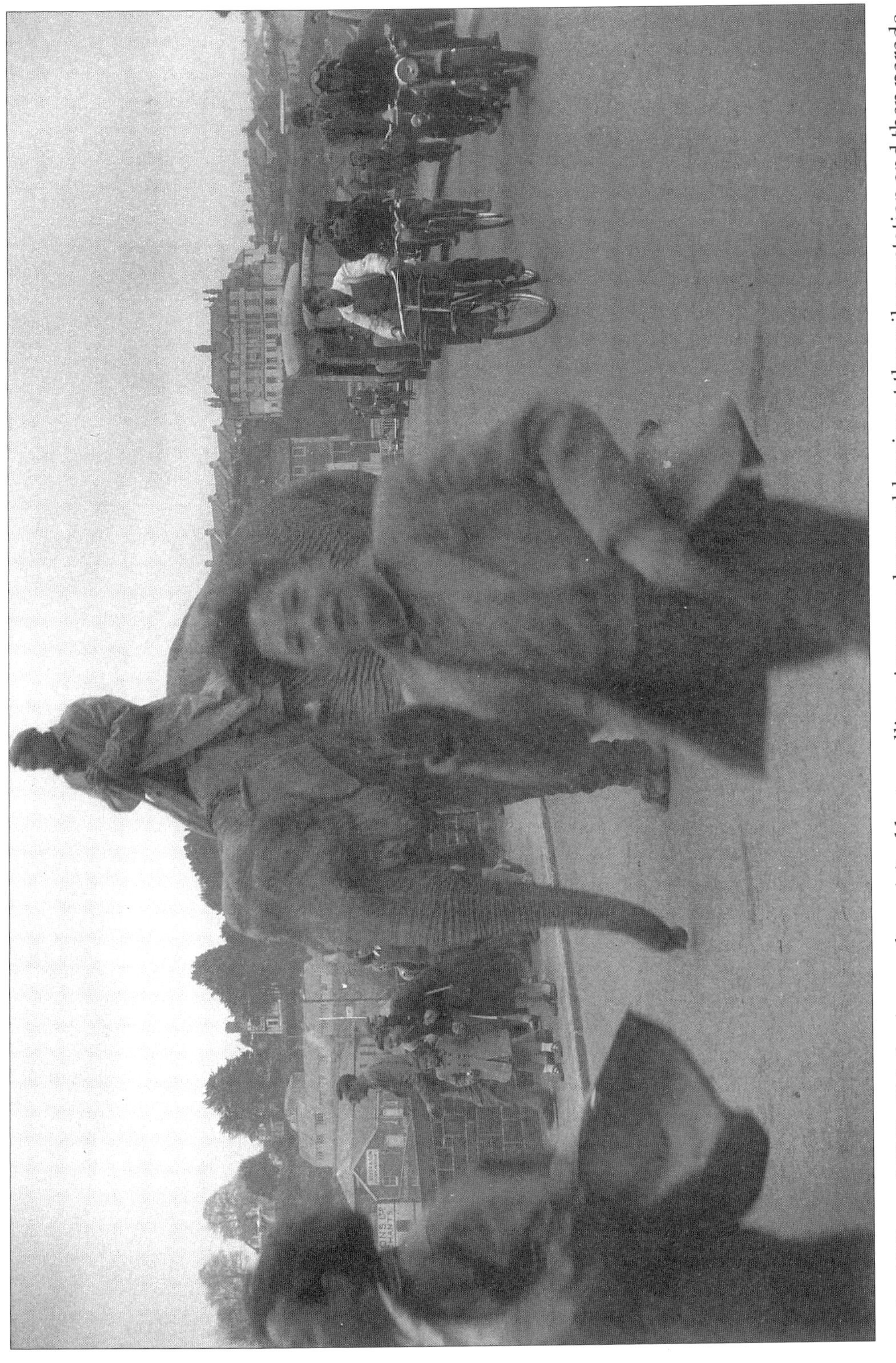

In the 1950s and 1960s Bideford was often visited by travelling circuses who would arrive at the railway station and then parade across the Bridge as a form of advertising and here from the early 1950s we see the incongruous sight of an elephant walking across the old Bridge - with a cheeky looking lad caught by the photographer just in front.

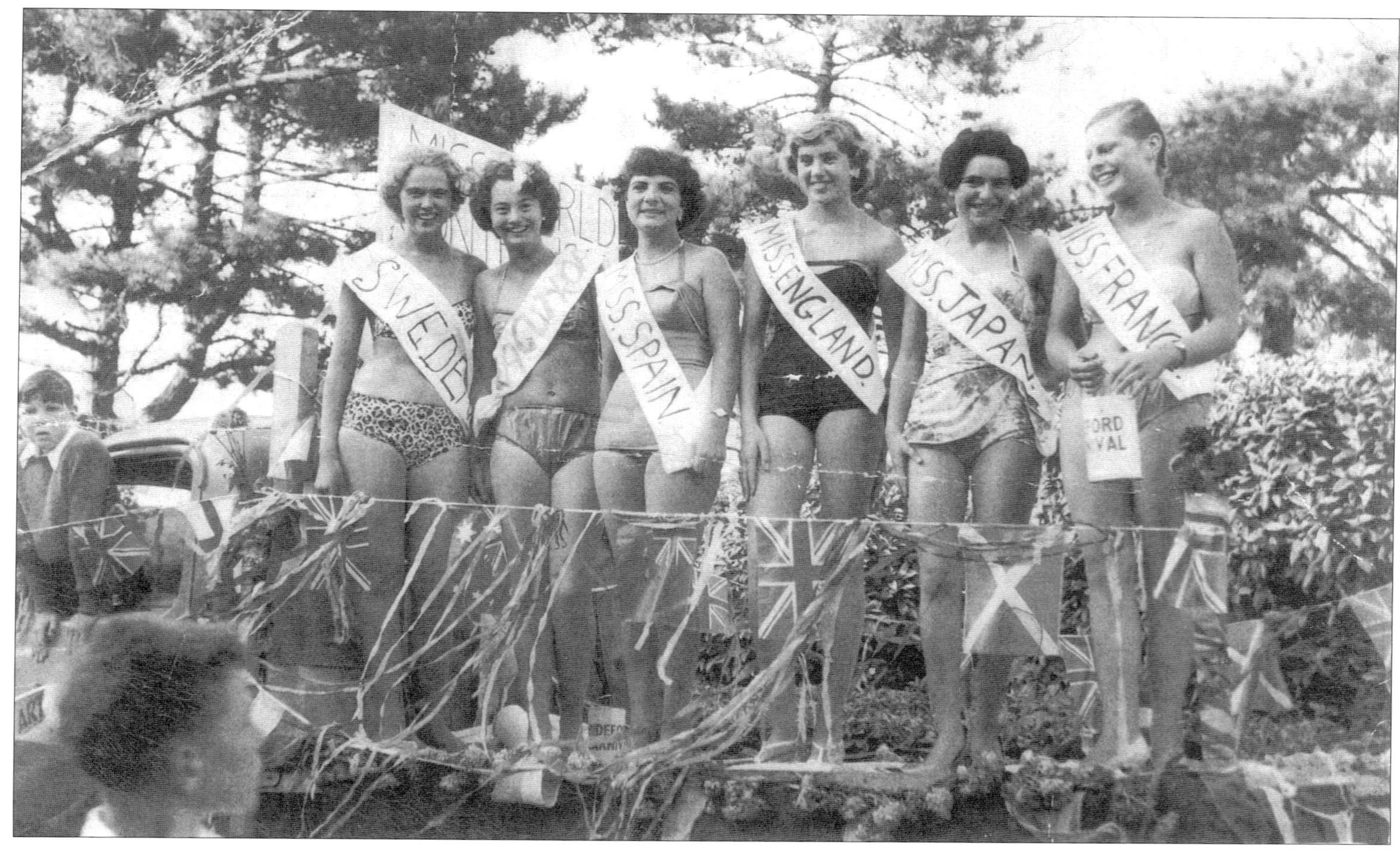

This photograph shows some very attractive entrants in the Bideford Carnival sometime around 1950. The 'sashes' may be home made but this 'Miss World' float was very popular with the onlookers who helped fill the collecting tins seen in the shot.

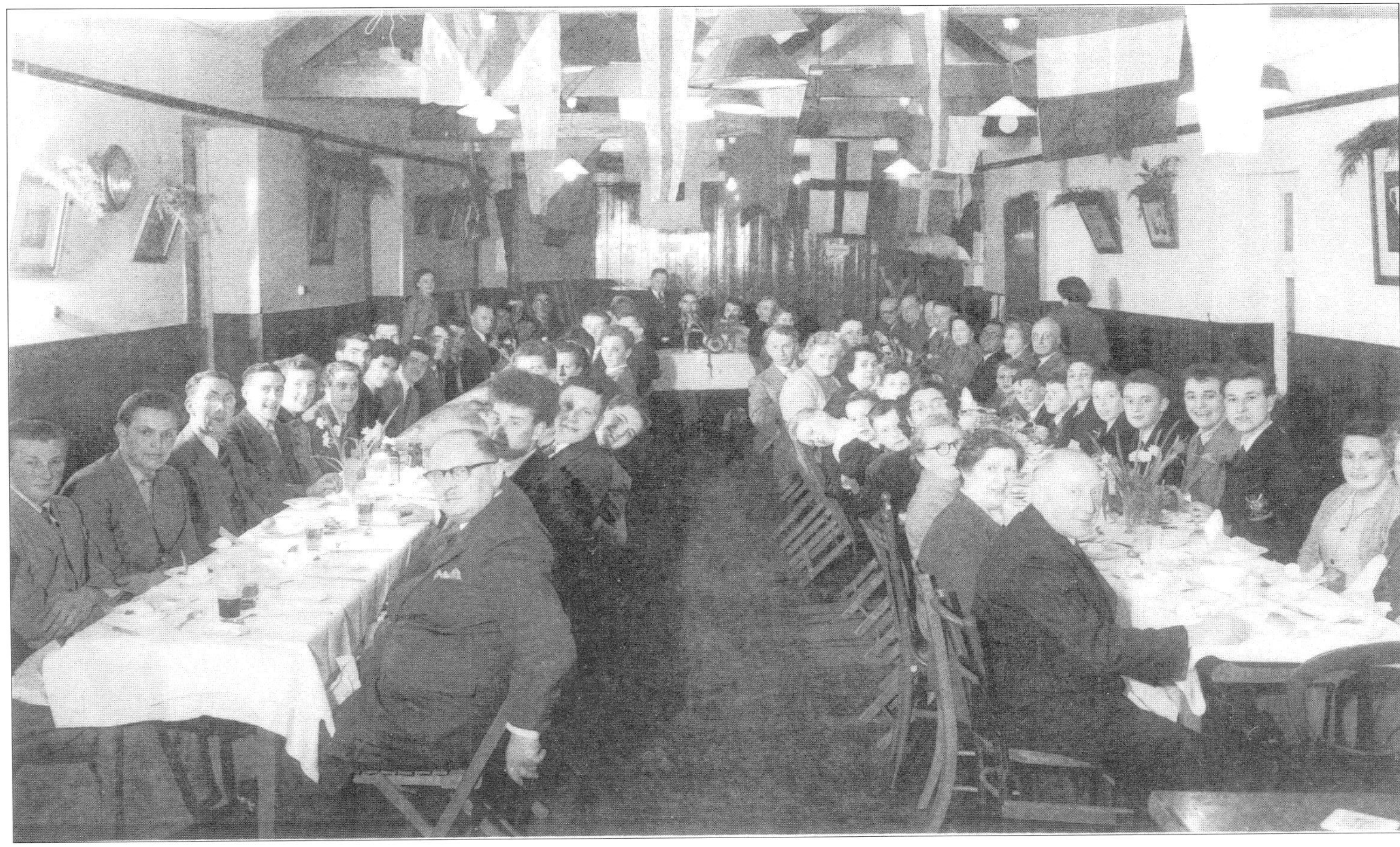

The cameraman seems to have got everyone to look towards him and has just said 'cheese' - hence this mostly smiling crowd. Taken at a Bideford 'Red's' Club Dinner in the 1950s it shows members of one of Bideford's two rowing clubs in a relaxed pose - and note the wide range of ages present - a feature still apparent today.

Above: Bideford carnival has always been a high point in the town's annual calendar and here we see some of the 'walking' entrants in the 1956 event. Note the politically incorrect 'Golly' and even the decorated dog. The winners were Elly Cox and Janet Watts who are standing next to the 'Golly'. *Below*: this comes from the same carnival and shows members of the town's Dancing School on their simply decorated but very effective float. There only seems to be one boy present he being dressed as a 'Captain' in charge of all his female 'sailors'. The photograph was taken in Park Lane in front of the Tennis Club whose site later became Marlborough Court.

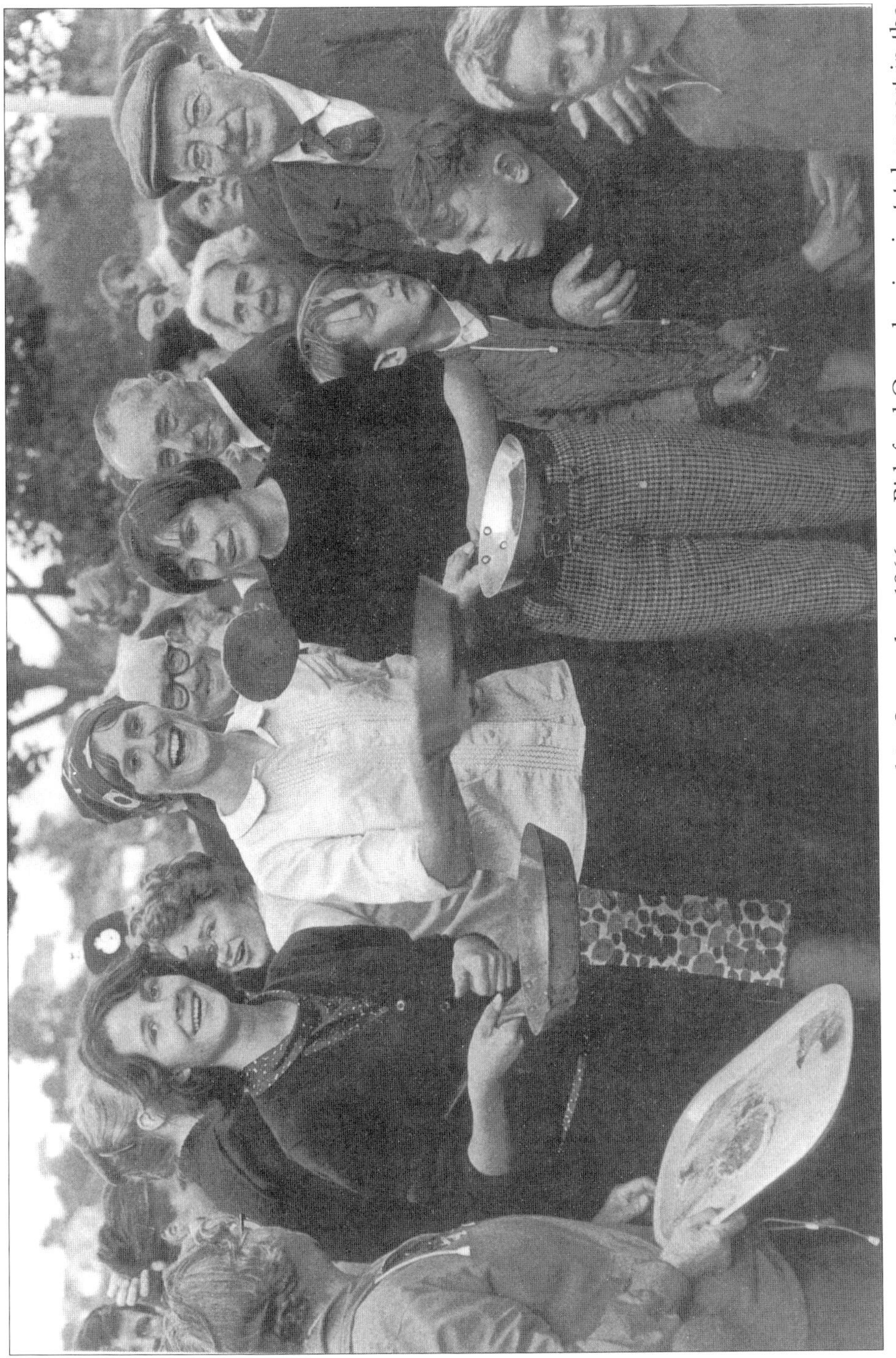

These happy looking pancake tossers were pictured in September 1966 on Bideford Quay having just taken part in the Regatta Week Pancake Race. The three contestants are, from left to right, Nicky Bissett, Caroline Veale and Anne Petherick. Ms. Veale, who came from Bristol, was the actual winner but the race was very close.

The Bideford Horse Show was always well supported and here we see the presentation of the championship cup at the Show in August 1956. The winner, on 'Whiskey' was Mrs.F.W.B.Smyth of Stoke Rivers and Mrs.R.D.D.Birdwood was doing the presenting.

Above: The Bridge Race, where runners attempted to race across the Bridge before St.Mary's clock finished striking 8 p.m. was very popular in the 1950s and 1960s. These two photographs show firstly the four competitors in 1961 starting off from the Town Hall whilst the second shows Chris Wood, a noted local athlete from the Bideford Amateur Athletic Club, receiving his winner's trophy in the Town Hall.

This happy looking group were pictured outside the Lamb Inn in Honestone Street sometime in the late 1950s or early 1960s. They were about to set out on a trip and a few of the names of the people have been recalled. On the extreme left is Jack Mallet whilst the lady seven along from him is Mrs.Shepherd whilst the lady in glasses is Mrs.Shortridge. The pub's landlady and landlord were Mrs. and Mr.Lascelles and they are the couple on the right - she in white bus driver's coat and he to her right. Reg Buckleigh is second from right.

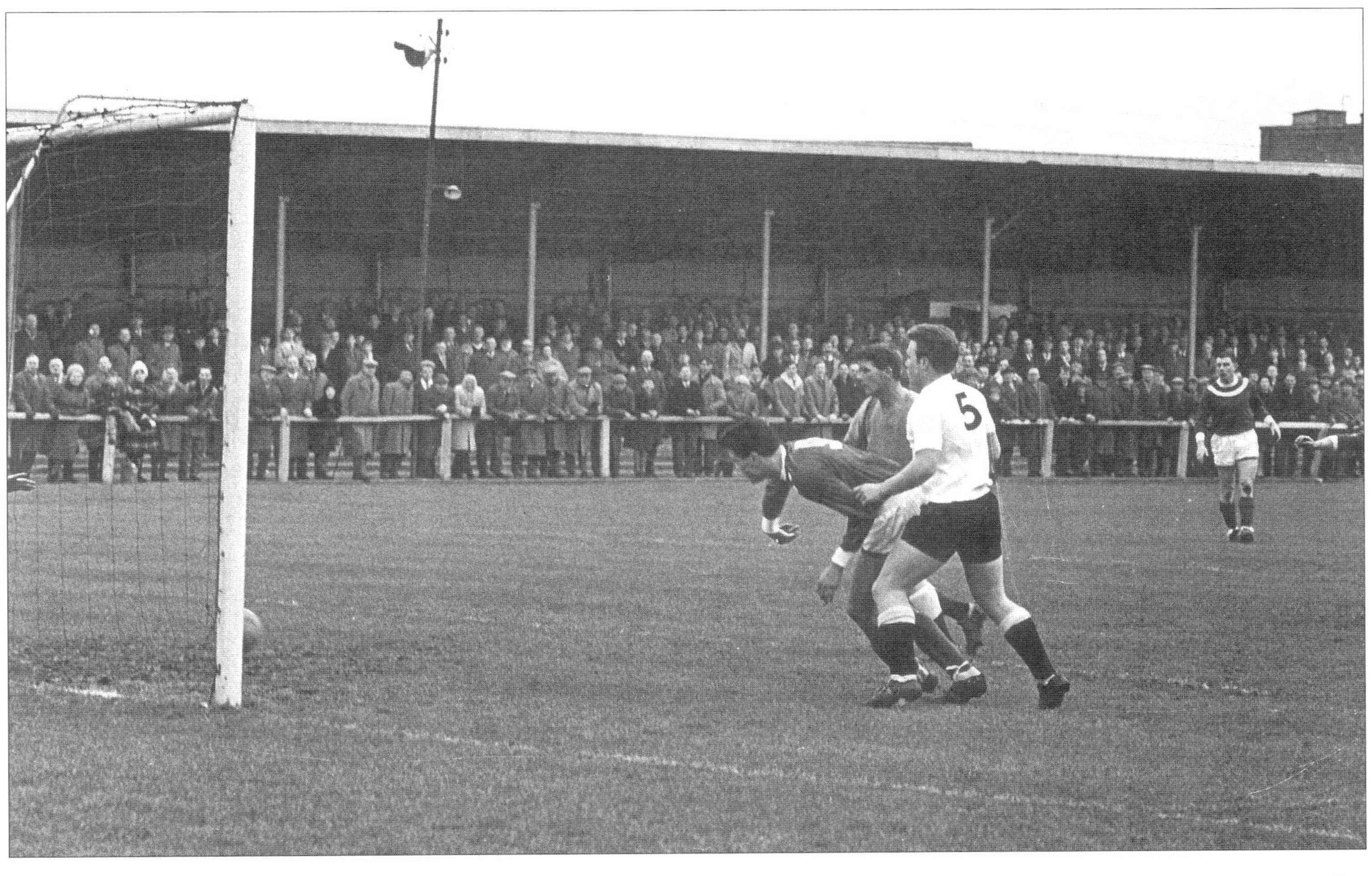

A local derby match in whatever sport between Barnstaple and Bideford always sees old rivalries rise up - and this particular football match from Boxing Day 1963 was no exception. Played at the Sports Ground it saw what was described as 'a mammoth £204' gate which was 'worth every penny'. Bideford were soon 2-0 down but a 'fantastic fight back' saw them eventually winning 3-2 with goals coming from Lol Chappell, Alan Marsh and John Penny.

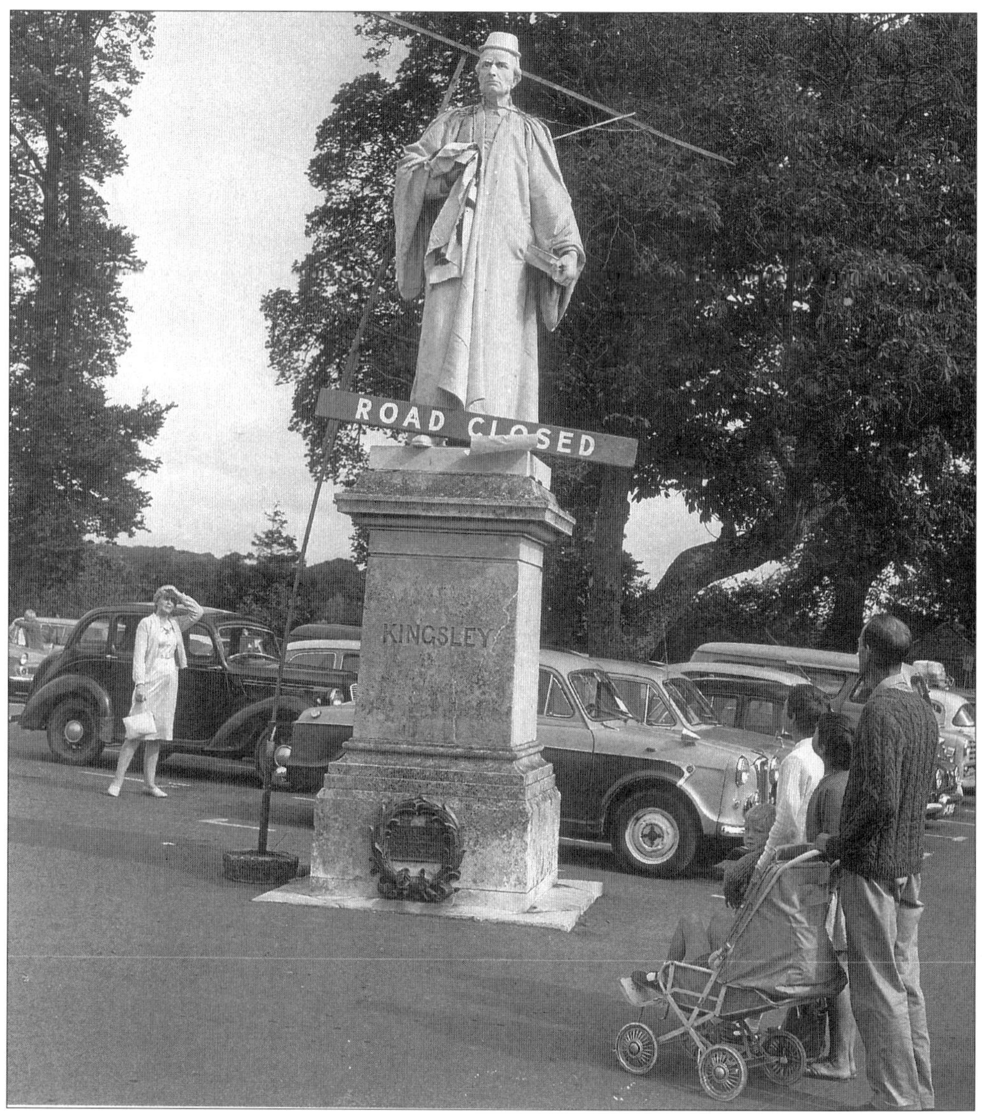

Above: Obviously this is the statue of Charles Kingsley at Bideford - but looking rather unusual. The picture records one of the 'japes' staged to mark the Bideford Schools' joint Rag Week in July 1967. Organised by Leslie Pickett of the Grammar School it raised over £200 for charity - with the 'Rag Queen' being Stanley Jones who, the North Devon Journal gravely reported, wore 'one of his mother's night gowns.'

Opposite: Bideford's Regatta Week has always been graced by the holding of a fair - even if its site has moved around a little - from the Pill, to around the Kingsley Statue, to the Rugby Club car park and back to the Statue area. This shot, taken from the top of the Post Office in the early 1970s records sideshows gathered around Kingsley.

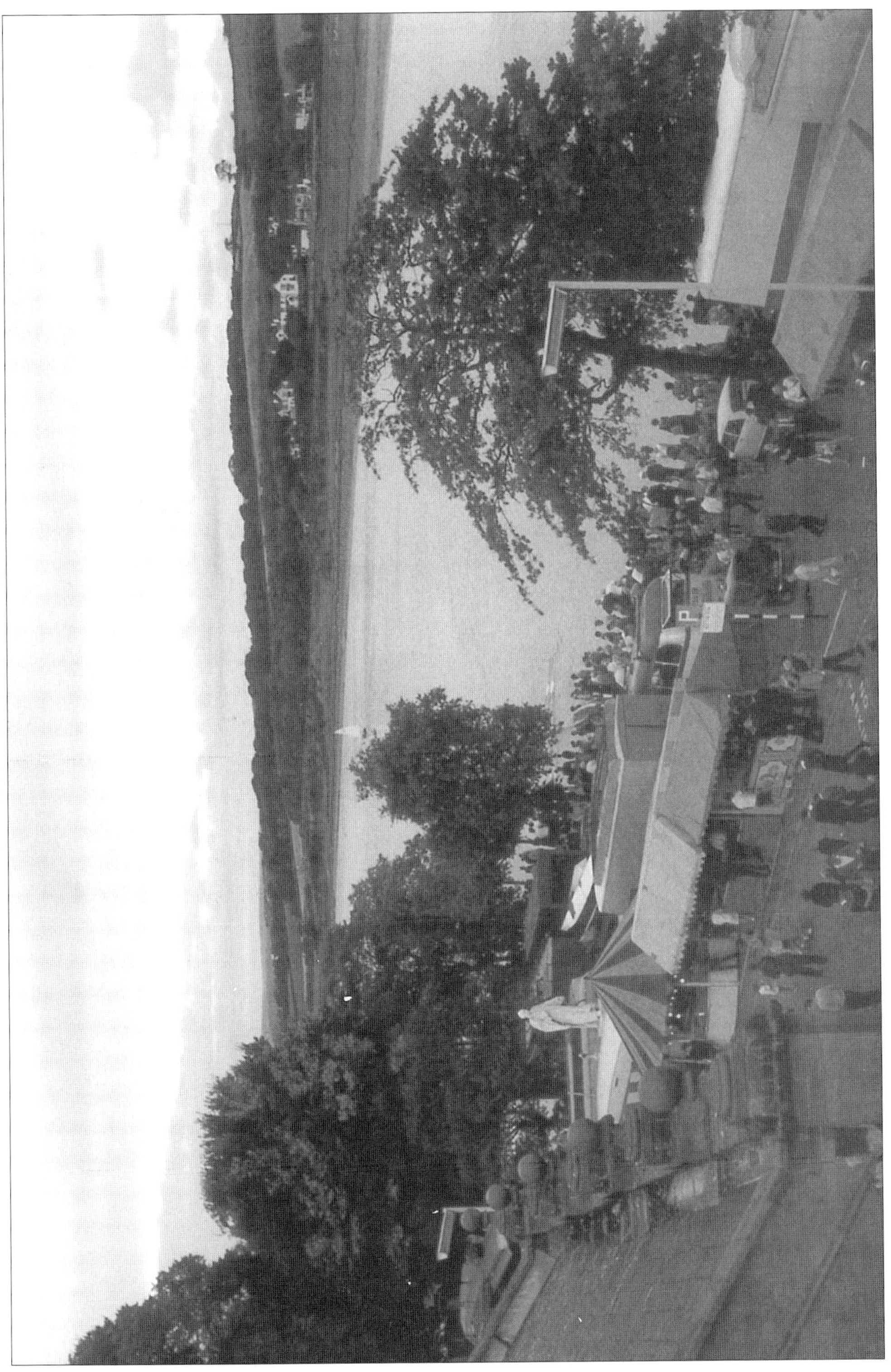

In June 1977 the Queen celebrated her Silver Jubilee - and her subjects throughout the country marked the event with street parties. Bideford wasn't to be left out and here we see one such party being held in Geneva Place on what was a very sunny and very happy day.

For many years the Bideford Water Carnival/Festival was a real occasion in the town and it has been resurrected of late. This shot dates from August 1980 and shows some of the rather odd home-made creations taking part in a raft race. The crowds are lining the old sloping river bank which has now been replaced by the Riverside car park's vertical stone walls.

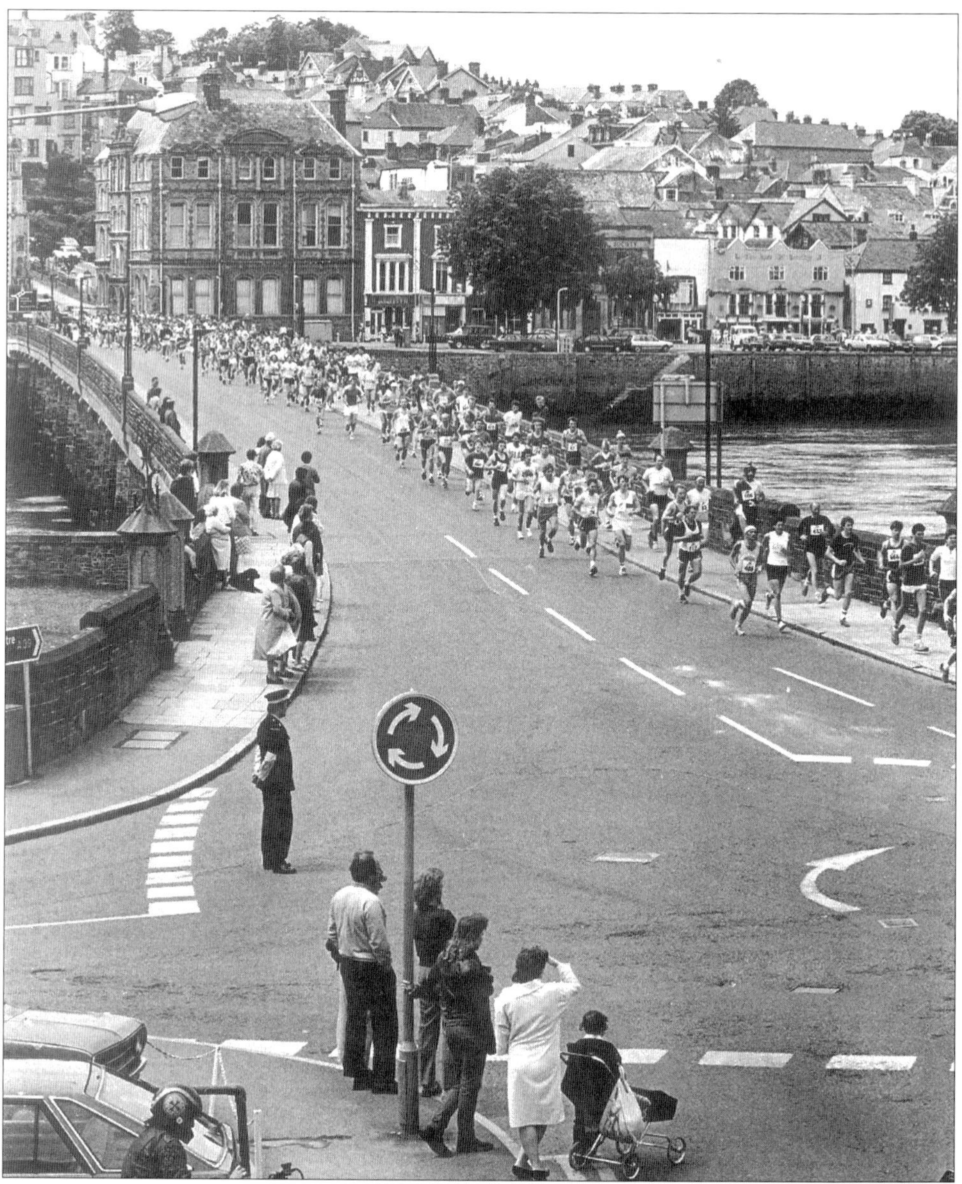

Above: The Bideford-Barnstaple Fun Run was a hugely popular event and here we see the vast field of 570 contestants crossing Bideford Bridge in June 1985 - the 5th annual race. The winner was Tony Collins from Winscott Farm, Holsworthy.

Opposite: This peculiar looking dinner party was being staged at Bideford's Football Ground in May 1985 by five of Bideford's long term supporters to mark a 'fine season'. The dinner-suited fans are (left to right) John Butler, Russell Laughton, Derek Read, Bob Hopkins and Brian Hopkins. The two boys standing behind them were Marcel Read and Jason Hopkins. Unfortunately the match they had come to see, a decider for the Western League championship, ended in a 2-0 defeat by Saltash.

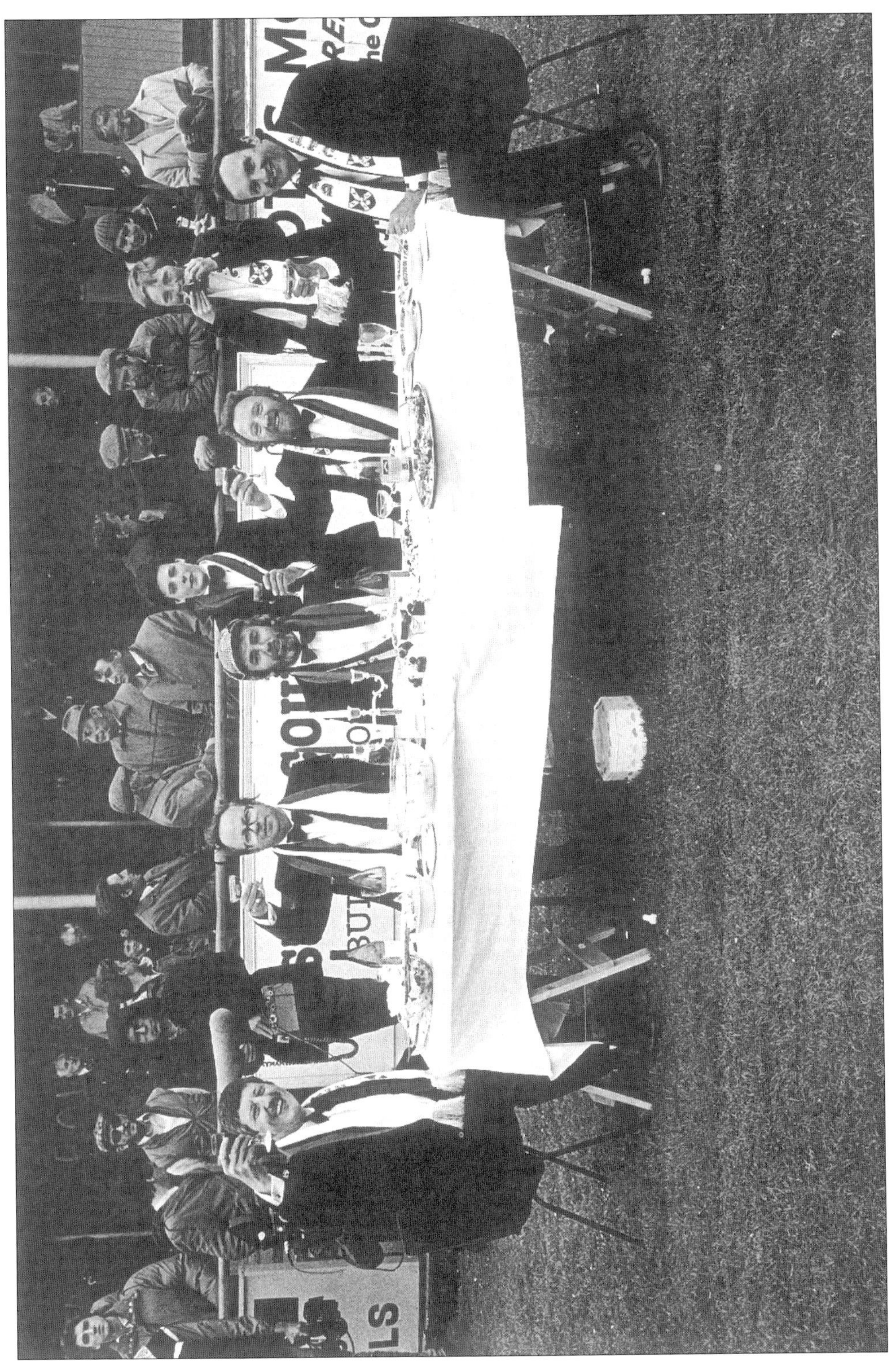

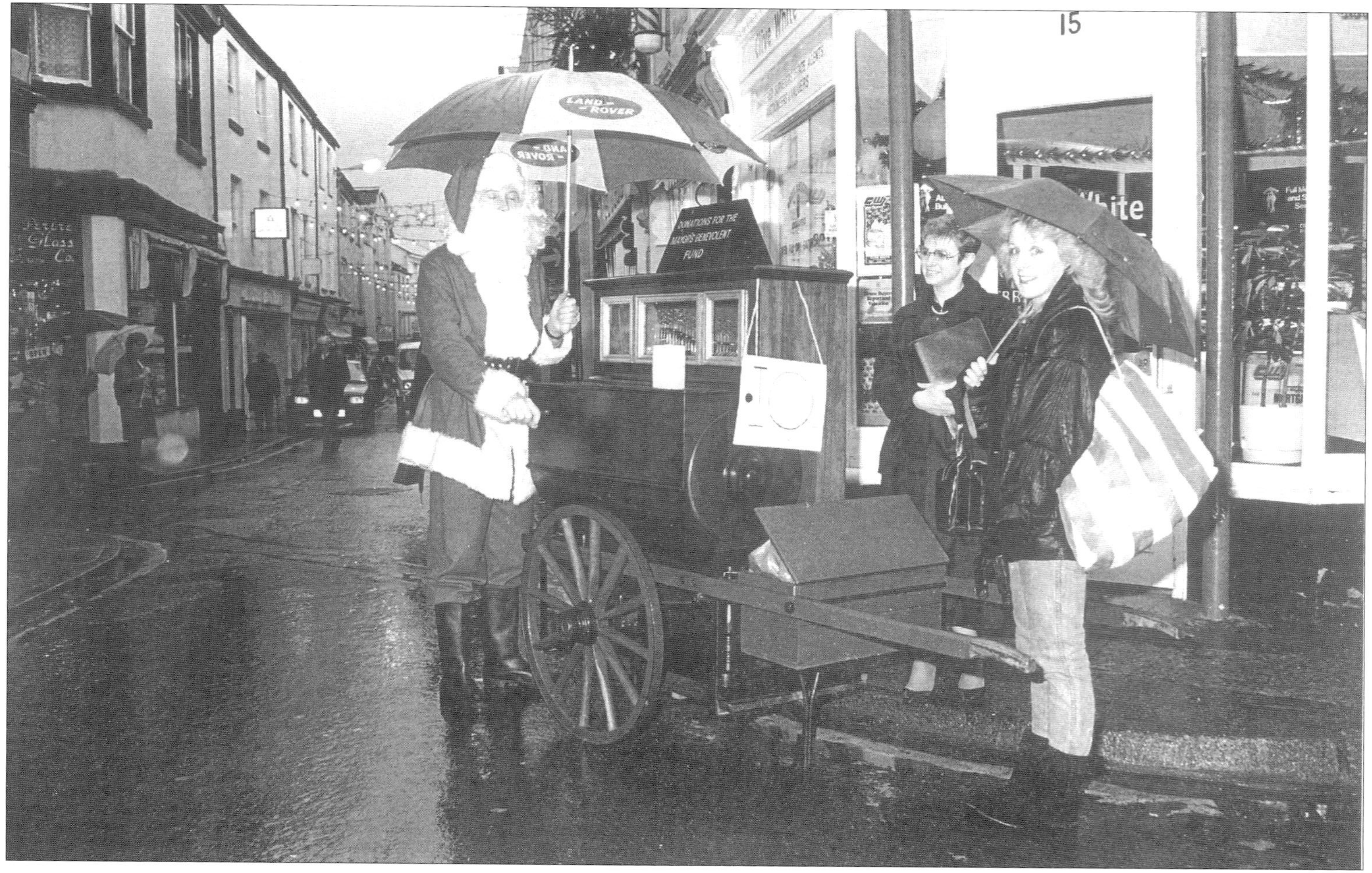

Barrel organs hadn't been played in Bideford's streets for many decades when this photograph was taken in December 1986. It shows local antique dealer John Biggs dressed as Father Christmas playing his restored organ in Mill Street whilst raising money for the Mayor's Benevolent Fund.

In 1992 the Milk Race completed one of its stages in Bideford and here we see the mass of cyclists hurtling down the Quay with a crowd looking on from behind crash barriers. Of course another bike race visited the town again in 2009 - when the crowds were appreciably larger.

Miscellaneous

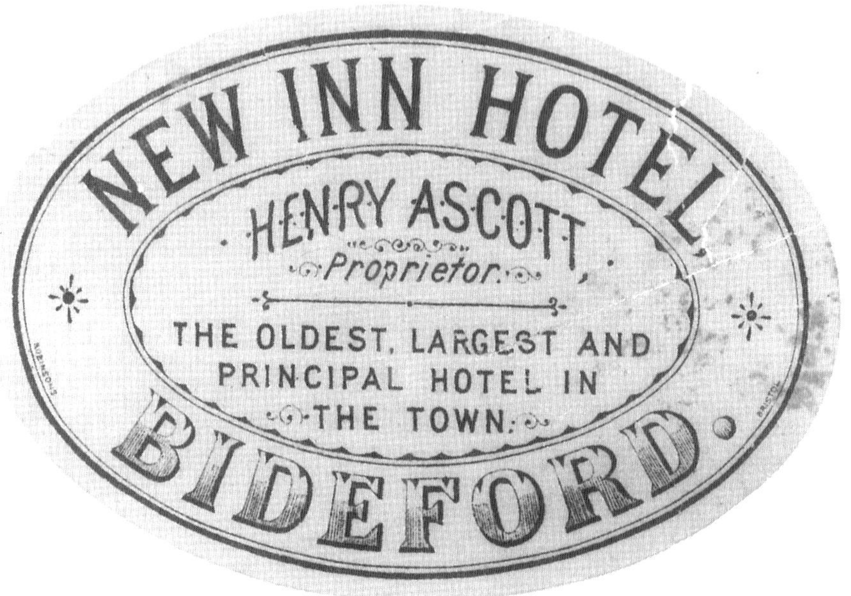

Above: For long the premier hostelry in Bideford the New Inn Hotel at the top of Bridge Street has recently been converted into flats. For many years at the end of the nineteenth and into the twentieth century it was run by Henry Ascott who himself published a small and very interesting booklet on his memories of Bideford. This picture shows a beer bottle label he had printed up to identify his own wares.

Opposite: Unfortunately I do not know what the occasion was for this charming group shot although given that some of the children are holding buckets and spades I would guess it was taken just prior to a charabanc trip to Westward Ho! The ladies' 'cartwheel' style hats date it to about 1905 and it was taken in Church Walk - St.Mary's is in the background.

Above: This very atmospheric shot shows the old building and chimney on the site of what is today Torridge District Council's headquarters at Riverbank House. The famous 'donkey' painting is on the wall and in the background is Chanter's Tower. The picture dates from around 1900 and seems to have been taken early in the morning to create a very artistic view.

Opposite: These young women were dressed in their Sunday best when they all attended W.Puddicombe's studio in the Strand to have their photograph taken. They were probably a Methodist chapel group with Marian Cock at the front on the left, second from right at the back was Katie Loveday Dennis and in the middle on the right with her hands on her lap was Edith Lamerton. They are all wearing what was high fashion around 1900-1905.

This wonderful collection of hats was seen at the wedding of Winifred Baker and Charles Stent in June 1906. They are standing outside Brunswick House which still stands at the bottom of Torridge Hill. Charles went on to run the main garage in Westward Ho! that was only recently demolished to provide space for new flats.

Although these youngsters are wearing military uniforms they were actually members of the Bideford Church Lad's Brigade - a militarised youth organisation run by the Church of England. This bugle band was photographed at a camp at Saunton just before the First World War.

Another picture of the Bideford Church Lad's Brigade this time taken, I think, in the grounds of the old Rectory at the top of High Street. One has to wonder how many of these young men and boys died in the carnage of the war that was soon to break out when this shot was taken?

West Bank School was founded in 1896 at Lansdowne Terrace and following rapid growth it moved into these handsome buildings on Belvoir Road. In 1955 the entire school moved to Sidmouth and its Bideford buildings were taken over by Grenville College which, in 2008, announced it was amalgamating with Edgehill College to form Kingsley College.

The old Stella Maris School in Bideford has now been transformed into flats and the site used for new houses but these two postcards show the interior of the school pre First World War when it was still known as the Ursuline Convent - and was so known 1904-29. Note the gas lights and the human sized mannequin in the left hand corner of the 'Studio' along with the selection of 'artistic' items the girls could practice sketching.

Above: The Girl Guides date their origin from 1911 though it was to be a few years before Bideford got its first group. It was formed at the West Bank School and was known as the '1st Bideford'. This group photograph dates from around 1926 and shows the members of that first unit. Back row, left to right; ?, M.Shapland, Muriel Goaman, Mudge. Next row; Ursula Radford, Patience Martin, Mary Fulford, Freda Trapnell, Ruby Yeo, Dorothy Farleigh, Barbara Harper, Isobel Clements. Next row; Amy Chope, Joy Rowe, Margaret Goaman, Angela Cabbon, Elsie Sutherland. Front row; ?, ?, Lulu Dymond, Enid Clements, Hilda Goaman. The two group leaders in the middle are Miss Beckwith and Miss Abbot the head mistress of the school.

Overleaf: The original of this shot was entitled 'Bideford Fire Brigade on the Clinton Estate'. It shows the 'Grenville' engine which the Brigade took delivery of in June 1927 and which attended the Plymouth blitz in 1941. It was said to be the last mobile unit operating in the city as its solid tyres did not catch fire and burst like her more modern equivalents!

Bideford's Workhouse at the top of Meddon Street dated from the 1830s and was always run by a Board of Guardians. These Guardians of the Poor were elected from the various parishes that made up the Bideford Union and here we see them at the rear of the Workhouse sometime in the late 1920s or early 1930s. On the front row second from right is Edward Lott, and three along is Elam Lott. The Workhouse nurse is on the extreme left.

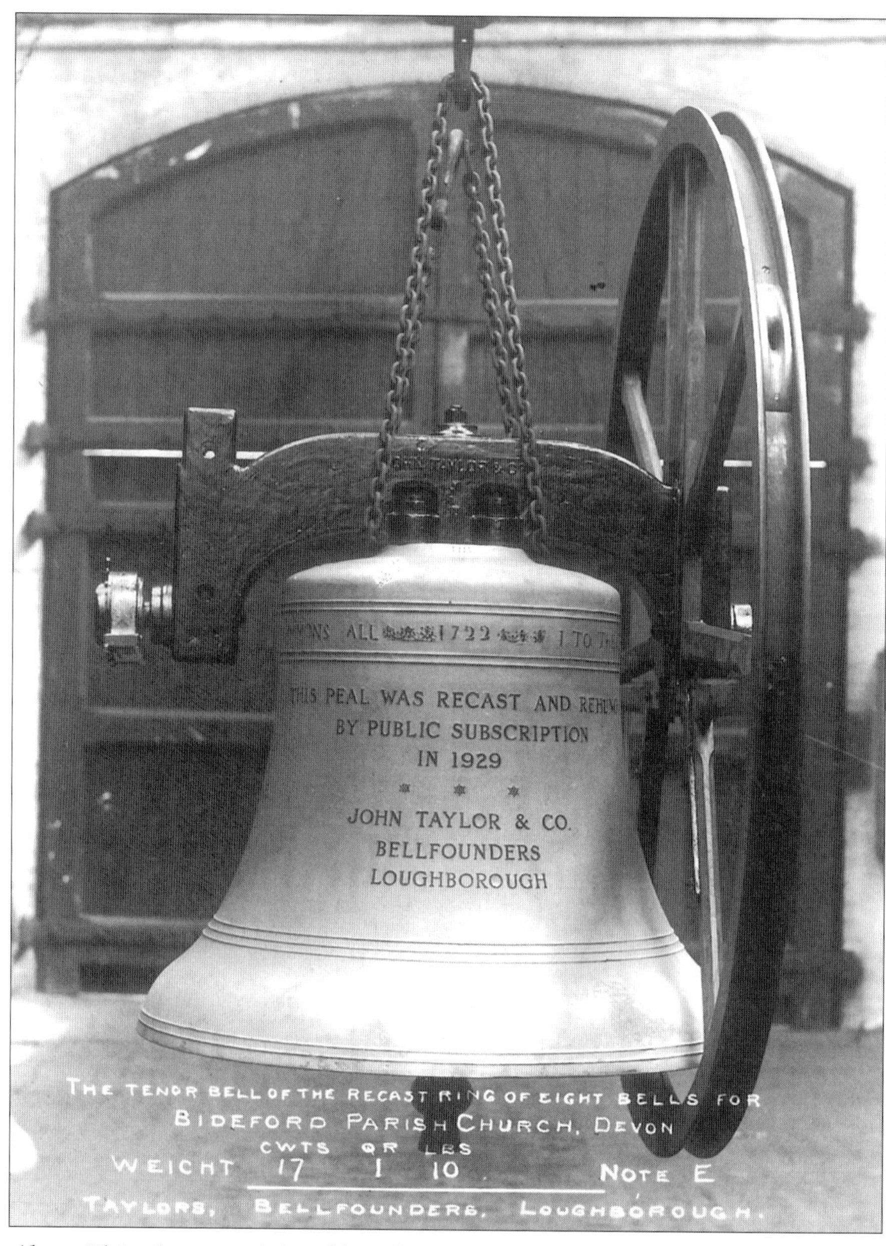

PEAL WAS RECAST AND
BY PUBLIC SUBSCRIPTION
IN 1929
JOHN TAYLOR & CO.
BELLFOUNDERS
LOUGHBOROUGH
THE TENOR BELL OF THE RECAST RING OF EIGHT BELLS FOR
BIDEFORD PARISH CHURCH, DEVON
CWTS QR LBS
WEIGHT 17 1 10 NOTE E
TAYLORS, BELLFOUNDERS, LOUGHBOROUGH.

Above: This photograph is self-explanatory. It shows one of St. Mary's bells at the Loughborough bell-founders' workshop of John Taylor & Co. - an object that many people have heard ringing but that few have seen.

Opposite: This picture was one of a series taken by S.R. Dark, photographer of Willet Street, in November 1939. It shows Alexandra Terrace in the Kenwith Valley when a series of storms led to the Kenwith stream bursting its banks and flooding the land behind the terrace. Today the dam and pumping station keeps the water in check.

The photograph on p.99 showed the initial stages of construction of the Church Institute in Lower Meddon Street in 1913 which housed the Church Infant School. This shot shows four of the pupils in the playground - which was on the roof owing to the lack of space anywhere else in the vicinity of the building. From left to right they were Norman Harding, Reggie Webb, Alec Short and Percy Vaughan

This wonderful group with the boys in shorts and the ties and the girls with bows in their hair and best dresses on was pictured in 1950 in the Church Institute in Lower Meddon Street. They were attending the Christmas Party held for the children of workers of the Southern National Bus Company.

Above: These houses still stand at the end of Lime Grove but when this postcard was produced in the early 1950s they still acted as a dormitory for West Bank School (later Grenville College). The inscription on the card reads 'The Holiday Fellowship' and I assume the houses were let to holidaymakers in the Summer break - much as Moreton House used to be let to Orthodox Jewish holiday groups in the 1990s

Opposite: The previous photograph showed the dormitories of West Bank School and here is a rather grainy photograph of one of the school's classrooms around 1904. Clearly the class sizes were small but how Spartan they look with their cast-iron and solid wooden desks.

This is a later group of the Church Lads Brigade. It probably dates from the late 1950s and although the military aspect of the organisation is still apparent they are nowhere near as 'militarised' as they appear in earlier photographs in this book. At this date the group was based in the Allhalland Street Drill Hall.

It is sometimes surprising how faces can look so different in old photographs. Look at the children in this one and they look so 1960s - the haircuts, clothes and just their appearance. The photograph dates from March 1964 and shows Mrs. L. Beech headmistress of Bideford Church Infants' School being presented with an electric fire to mark her relocation to another school in Hampshire, whilst the vicar is the Reverend T.Derwent Davies.

The Fire Service in Bideford has a long and proud history. This group shot was taken in 1969 or 1970 and shows the men lined up in front of one of the engines in their Old Town headquarters. They are, back row, left to right, Michael Hacker, ?, Kenny Upton, Albert Blackmore, John Hare, Ron Hammett, Jack Heywood, Maurice Copp, Alan Persicoe, Jimmy Weeks, Chris Wood, Front row, Reg Colwell, Sub-Officer Clifford Coates, Station Officer Tommy Trick, Leading Fireman Teddy Webb, Leading Fireman Lou Rowsen.

Above: Edgehill College opened in Bideford in 1884 and since then the girls have been closely connected to the life of the town. In 1975 a group of them arranged a three-legged sponsored walk in aid of a charity for the homeless. They are seen here setting out from the College in rather wet weather.

Overleaf: This scrum of people gathered in Bideford's Mill Street in March 1983 had come to try and catch a glimpse of actor Johnny Briggs alias 'Mike Baldwin' of television's 'Coronation Street' when he came to town to open a new clothes shop called What Not. He arrived nearly an hour late having been delayed by 'fog and caravans' and was greeted with a huge cheer - to be followed by a mass stampede into the shop by people keen to get his autograph. Such is the attraction of the soap star.

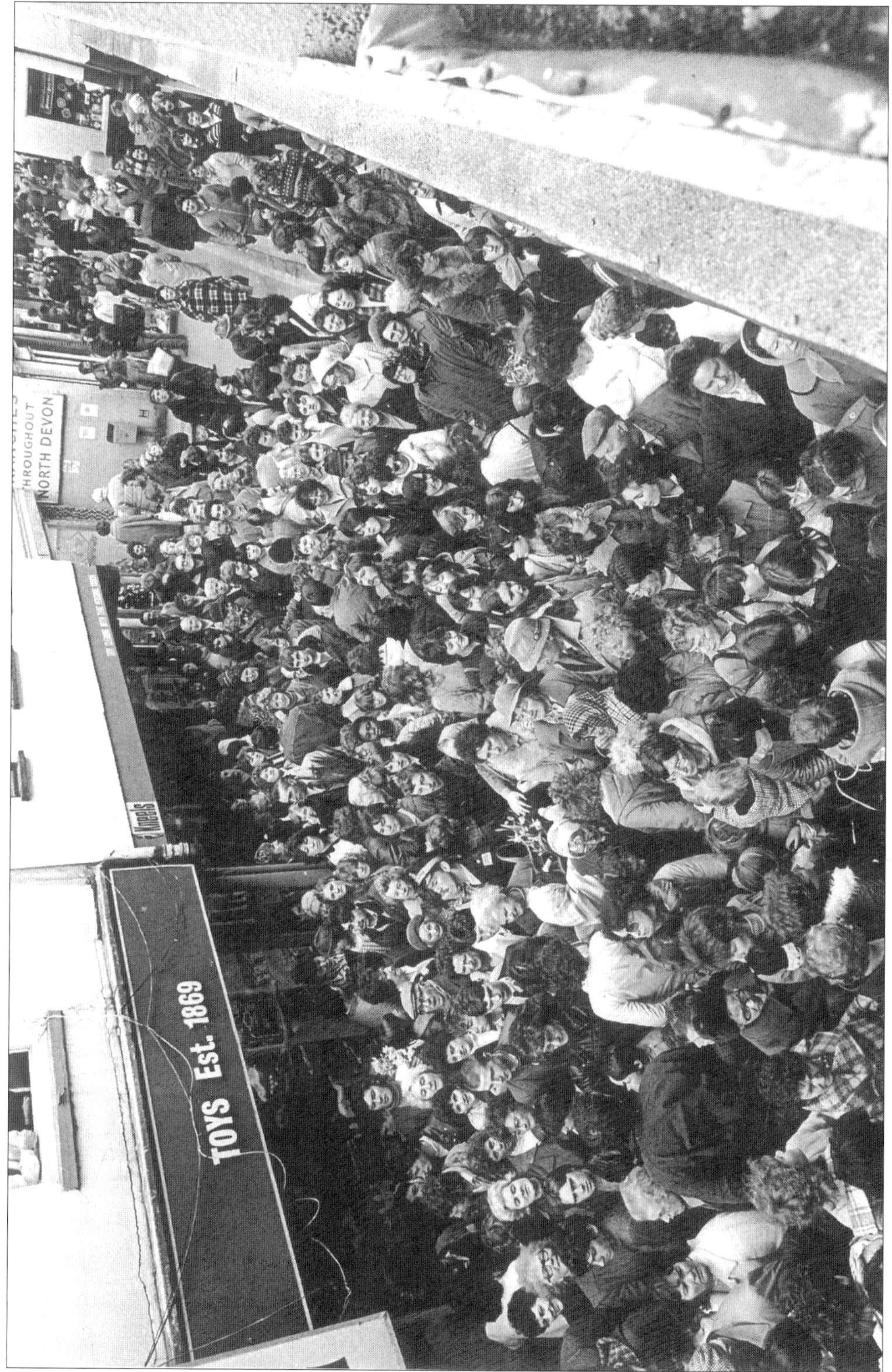
TOYS Est. 1869
THROUGHOUT
NORTH DEVON

For some years now the churches in Bideford have combined to stage a march of 'witness' to mark Good Friday. This photograph shows the event in April 1984 when the procession was passing along North Road - not one of the streets in Bideford that has been photographed that often.

Love them or hate them there seem to have been slowly deteriorating boats moored on the mud banks on the eastern side of the river for many years now. In 1985 Torridge district council decided to clean up the worst of them and this photograph shows workmen filling skips at low tide with some of the rubbish.

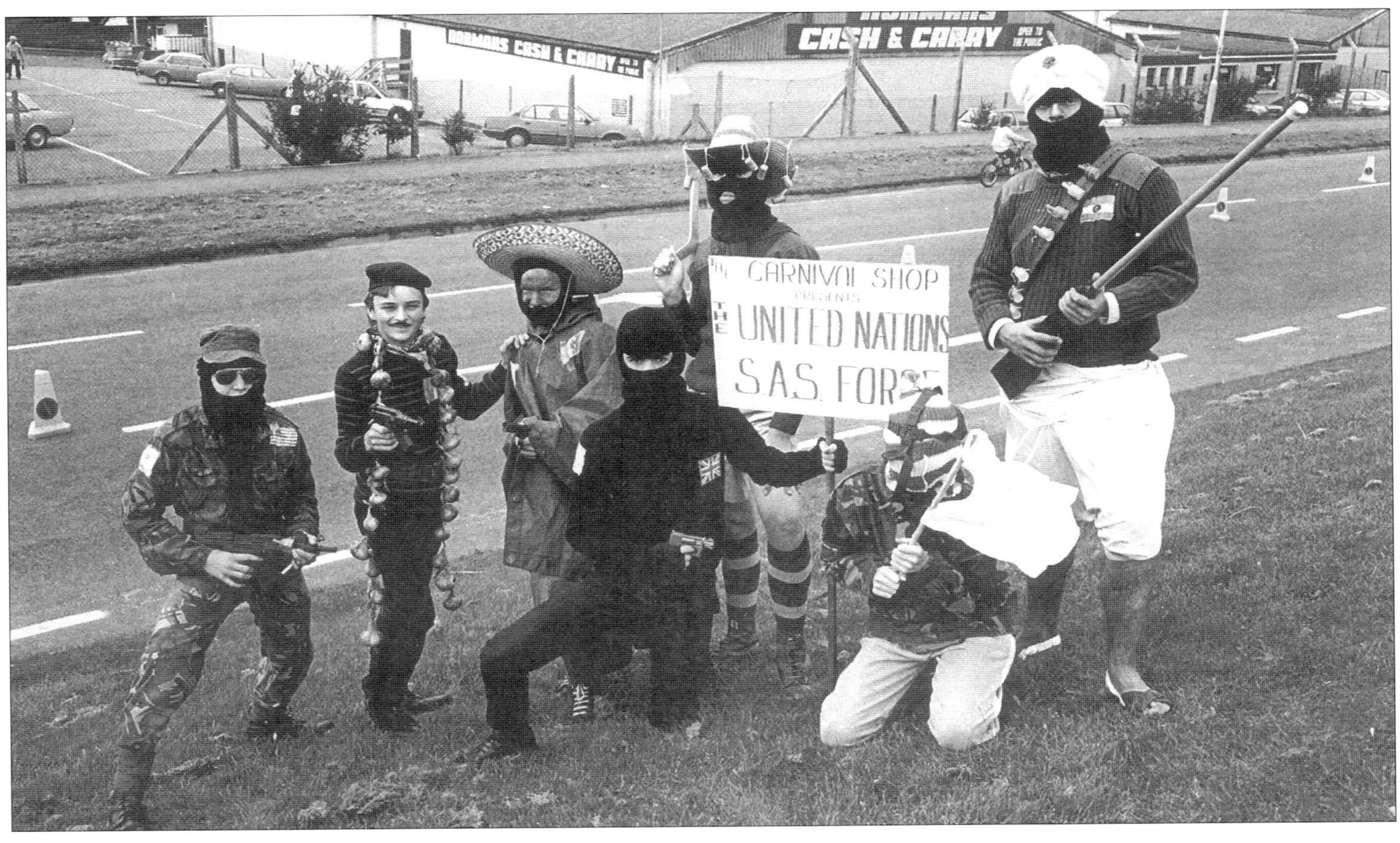

This rather odd looking group appeared at the town's Carnival in September 1986. They called themselves the United Nations SAS Force and were made up of lads from the King's Arcade Carnival Shop. In the 1980s this long gone arcade occupied what is now the premises for Caesar's Palace nightclub. Notice the old Norman's Supermarket behind the group which too has gone to be replaced by a modern housing estate. I am told the chain link and barbed wire fence surrounding the store was left over from the wartime US military base/displaced people's camp that used to stand here.

For much of the 1970s and 80s Bideford's growth was restricted by a 'sewage embargo' placed on the town by South West Water. Owing to a lack of sewage capacity virtually no new houses could be built. In November 1986 SWW announced they were to build a fine screening plant - which meant that untreated sewage would still be poured into the Torridge at Bideford. To register their outrage a group of local Green Party members marched along the Quay carrying a mock 'coffin' to mark the 'death' of the river. Since then of course full treatment has been introduced. In the photograph I am on the left with my young daughter Jessica behind me whilst the fourth back is Bill Thornton - after whom Thornton Close on Londonderry is named.

The final photograph links history to the future. Taken in August 1987 in the old Rose of Torridge cafe on the Quay, it shows some of the team of women (and one man) who, under the leadership of Mary Rogers, were working on a tapestry showing the 'adventurous times and achievements of contemporary and post-Elizabethan Westcountrymen.' This rival to the Bayeaux Tapestry was due to take two years to finish before going on display - a nice link across the years.

Lazarus Press
Bideford